The Resilience of Christianity
in the Modern World

❖ ———————————————————————————— ❖

SUNY Series in Religion, Culture, and Society

Wade Clark Roof, Editor

The Resilience of Christianity in the Modern World

Joseph B. Tamney

State University of New York Press

"Constructive Greed" © 1974 by *The Muncie Star.* Reprinted with permission.

"Pope, Visiting Polish Factory, Proclaims Conditions Unsafe" © 1987 by the *New York Times* Company. Reprinted by permission.

Published by
State University of New York Press, Albany

© 1992   State University of New York

For information, address State University of New York
Press, State University Plaza, Albany, N.Y. 12246

Production by M. R. Mulholland
Marketing by Fran Keneston

Library of Congress Cataloging-in-Publication Data

Tamney, Joseph B.
     The resilience of Christianity in the modern world / Joseph B.
     Tamney.
          p.   cm. — (SUNY series in religion, culture, and society)
     Includes bibliographical references and index.
     ISBN 0–7914–0821–3 (alk. paper) . — ISBN 0–7914–0822–1 (pbk. :
alk. paper)
          1. Sociology, Christian. 2. Christianity—20th century.
     I. Title. II. Series
     BT738. T25   1992
     306.6'3—dc20
                                                                   90–22086
                                                                   CIP

10 9 8 7 6 5 4 3 2 1

Contents

Tables

❖ ——————————————————————————— ❖

Preface

❖ ——————————————————————————————— ❖

My purpose is to understand what makes a specific religion popular in a particular time and place. Popularity is a broad term. Being popular can mean simply being accepted by people, being liked, or being very well liked by everyone. I am interested in a holistic theory that can explain everything from the mere use of a religious label such as "Catholic" to a deep commitment to a religious way of living.

Among social scientists, a category to which I belong, a dominant scholarly thesis had been that modernization led to secularization; the interpretation of the latter ranged from a lessening of religious influence to the demise of religion. In short, we generally believed that as the West modernized, religious popularity waned. But confidence about the truth of this idea has declined more than religious popularity has. In the United States, the 1980s seemed to see a religious renaissance. Jerry Falwell made news with his Moral Majority organization. The Catholic bishops criticized national policy—first concerning disarmament, then, about the economy. In its original, simplistic terms, the modernization-secularization thesis is no longer useful. In this work I incorporate this thesis into a more elaborate theory that, I believe, better fits the facts.

Religion is a set of rules for living that are meant to bring us into harmony with a superhuman will or order of some kind. A religion has been part of every known society, which is easy to understand because social life everywhere evokes the same problems, and it is reflection on these problems that moves us toward religion.

> What is man? What is the meaning, the purpose of life? What is the moral good and what is sin? Whence suffering and what purpose does it serve? Where lies the path to true happiness? What is the truth about death, judgement, and retribution beyond the grave? What, finally, is that ultimate inexpressible mystery which encompasses our existence: whence do we come, and where are we going? (From the proceedings of the Catholic Vatican Council II, quoted in Rossano 1981:96)

Leaving aside the references to sin and judgement, such questions are part of the human condition and serve as the fountainhead of religious interest. The universality of such questions guarantees a certain degree of religious popularity in any society.

Just as it is true that religion is everywhere, it is equally true that religious popularity has varied over time and from place to place at any one time. My theoretical goal is to understand such variation. In the Introduction, I attempt to unravel the complex relationships between modernization and religion. The net effect of modernization does seem to be a lessened place for religion. The Introduction concludes with the presentation of a theoretical framework for understanding religious popularity in a modern context. The remainder of the book is an effort to use this framework in order to understand the resilience of Christianity in the modern world.

A key aspect of this framework is that a religion's popularity is shaped by its response to three cultural sets of beliefs and values that have appeared during the course of modernization—namely, the libertarian, socialist, and countercultural ideational sets (with *set* referring to a number of beliefs and values that are neither a congeries nor a code, but are closer to the latter). These ideational sets have become the bases for social movements, which have challenged churches in various ways. Chapters 1 through 5 examine specific cases of the interaction of such movements and Christianity with the purpose of showing how the interaction is affecting the popularity of this religion.

While the Introduction offers a broad overview of the first several thousand years of Western history, the rest of the book examines in detail how Christianity and modern ideas are affecting each other. Religious popularity is limited by the nature of modern society; within those limits, such popularity results from the way specific religions react to modern ideas. In the Conclusion, the theoretical framework is reformulated and extended on the basis of the material presented in Chapters 1 through 5. I end with a summary of why Christianity is resilient and of the processes that seem to be limiting the appeal of Christianity in the modern world.

Introduction:
Modernization and the
Resilience of Christianity

❖ ——————————————————————————————— ❖

While the argument that modernization produces secularization is still defended, it has increasingly been criticized (Hadden 1987). It is especially difficult to convince Americans that religion is losing influence because almost all of them say that they believe in God and a majority belong to churches. American experience does not seem to support the modernization-secularization thesis. However, based on an analysis of modernization and its consequences, it is argued in this Introduction that modernization has forever lessened religious popularity. Religion will never again play as great a role as it did in earlier times.

It is also true, however, that religion remains important to people and that churches are struggling to become more powerful parts of society. Modern history is not simply the inevitable and complete decline of religion. Therefore, after discussing how historical changes have brought about secularization, a broader theoretical framework is presented that incorporates the insights of secularization theory but also opens the way to understanding the obvious vitality of religion in modern society.

To begin, however, it is necessary to bring intellectual order into the wide-ranging discussion of secularization. In succeeding pages, the various aspects of secularization are differentiated, and the social processes accounting for the appearance of each aspect are described. Once the modernization-secularization argument is clear, the ground is prepared for a discussion of an alternative theory that gives structure to this book.

Compared With What?

To study change, we must ask the basic question: With whom do we compare the present society? In this essay, two kinds of comparison are made. First, modern society (i.e., contemporary Western society) will be compared with traditional society. Many of the following remarks are applicable to non-Western societies, but the examples and analyses focus on the Western or European experience. Second, comparisons will be made between present society and earlier periods of European civilization. As is customary, it is assumed that this civilization began during the period of classical Greek culture, declined during the Dark Ages, reemerged in the late Middle Ages, and then evolved into contemporary Western civilization. The Western modernization process, then, can be described in terms of changes that began during the sixth century B.C. in the Greek city-states and in terms of the changes that have occurred in the West since the Dark Ages.

Secularization

According to *Webster's New World Dictionary* (Second College Edition), to *secularize* means to change from religious to civil use, to deprive of religious character, influence, or significance, or to convert to secularism. In turn, *secularism* means a system of doctrines and practices that disregard or reject any form of religious faith and worship. The basic meaning of *secularization* is that religion loses social significance. The extreme case would be a completely secularist society—i.e., one without religion. But secularization is a complex matter and exists in varying shades. I will discuss this subject under five headings: secularism, desacralization, structural differentiation, privatization, and commitment to Christianity.

Secularism

Given the age of our species, secularism must be considered new, but its origin goes back to the beginning of Western civilization. European secularism began with the sophists of classical Greece, who were agnostics and believed that humans could never hope to settle the truth of religion. Supposedly, it was their awareness of religious diversity that led the sophists to conclude that all religions were a matter of custom and thus relative to time and place (Thrower 1971:30). Sophist-like arguments reappeared during the Italian Renaissance (Gibson 1955:524–25) and have remained part of Western culture.

Secularism did not become culturally significant in Western history until about the seventeenth century. According to Weintraub: "Whatever else the Enlightenment was, it surely was also the moment when Western man, for the first time since antiquity, fully faced up to the tremendous task of justifying his existence by creating a secular civilization" (1978:294). But these "Western men" were few in number, members of the elite, literally men, and not truly secularists (Hobsbawm 1962:259; Baumer 1960).

Rather than being secularists, seventeenth-century skeptics leaned toward latitudinarianism. They "boiled Christianity down to a few simple 'essentials' often including not much more than belief in Jesus as the Messiah and belief in a righteous life...." (Baumer 1960:108–9). Like the sophists, these skeptics were influenced by their awareness of other cultures, both contemporary and ancient. Europeans were learning about Islamic, Indian, and Chinese civilizations. Between 1660 and 1740, for example, more than five hundred books appeared about the Orient. The questioning attitude was further stimulated by the proliferation of Christian denominations all claiming to be the true form of this religion. Thus, as in classical Greece, religious diversity spurred the development of the skeptical tradition (Baumer 1960:98–104).

What gave added importance to skepticism in the early modern period was the scientific revolution and its espousal of the open, questioning mind (MacIntyre 1969:8–11). The scientific frame of mind was uncomfortable with accepting irrefutable beliefs such as the Christian belief in God. Empirical methods became an alternative to religious works as sources of truth. Science and the early philosophical speculations that preceded it revealed a 'new nature,' one that seemed to run without God's intervention.

The increasing awareness of diverse religions and the development of science initially aroused only a desire to simplify Christianity, to reduce it to its core, but these two cultural changes eventually led to the growth of deism. The French Revolution, which attempted to deinstitutionalize Christianity and replace it with a religion of nature and reason "written in the hearts of everyone," illustrated the new religious consciousness (Baumer 1960:52). But even eighteenth-century skeptics were not anti-religious, just anti-Christian, and this Voltairean posture did not spread to the masses (Vidler 1961:13).

It is in the present century that understanding of other religions and cultures is diffusing throughout modern societies. People around the world are becoming more aware of and informed about the universal religions such as Buddhism, Islam, and Christianity. Colonialism, world wars, international trade, multinational corporations, and international tourism have contributed to this growing religious sophistication. Moreover, religious institutions are ensuring that their wisdom books are being translated into more languages and are more readily available to the masses. All of this means that average individuals are becoming increasingly aware of the religious pluralism in the world. Similarly, the spread of public education, especially beyond grammar school, during the twentieth century has meant the exposure of masses of people to science for the first time.

In addition, culture has been affected by a very recent event in human history—namely, the popularization of social science thinking and findings. To understand the importance of the social sciences, we must remember how firmly established the experiential basis of religious belief was, especially as we go back in history.

In traditional society, religious belief was confirmed in ritual experience. Geertz (1966:32) tried to substantiate this argument with a discussion of a Balinese ritual during which not only the primary actors playing mythical figures, but also dozens of spectators, become possessed by one or another demon. "Mass trance, spreading like a panic, projects the individual Balinese out of the commonplace world in which he usually lives into that most uncommonplace one in which Rangda and Barong live." As Geertz (1966:34) wrote: "To ask, as I once did, a man who has *been* Rangda whether he thinks he is real is to leave oneself open to suspicion of idiocy." We can readily understand that people who had experienced a quite different form of themselves could believe that they had experienced the unseen world of religion—could, that is, until the development of behavioral sciences cast severe doubt that such transformations had anything to do with the non-natural. True, experiences similar to the Balinese one occur today during religious rituals, and they no doubt help to substantiate the beliefs of their members. In some Christian groups, people still 'become' the deity, or at least come into direct contact with 'him'. But the work of scientists such as Geertz (and, before him, Sigmund Freud and Emilé Durkheim) offer alternative explanations to the religious one for what happens during rituals. These scientists have emphasized the existence of nonconscious processes that can, quite naturally, produce seemingly unexplainable occurrences. Social science does not (indeed, cannot) prove that supposed religious experiences are purely natural, but social scientific studies have raised this possibility and thus may evoke doubts in reflective people about their apparent religious experiences, if not a redefinition of them as simply secular phenomenon.

Specific studies in the sociology of religion (such as this one) have their own kind of impact on culture. We know that our beliefs and values are affected by personal biography and social history. The modern critical consciousness is related to the realization that not only personal views but also religious doctrines are conditioned by historical and social conditions. The social sciences, then, not only raise questions about the experiential foundation of religious beliefs, but these sciences promote a questioning of the veracity of all intellectual products—including religious doctrines.

It is mainly in the present century, then, that secularism has spread across social classes. The causes for this seem to be the popular awareness of religious diversity, the scientific method, and social science findings. In the twentieth century, it became acceptable to be irreligious: "In the existence of irreligion...manifesting itself to some extent in all social strata and having a degree of social and legal recognition, modern societies appear to be unique" (Campbell 1971:5).

In fact, the prevalence of atheists and agnostics varies greatly among Western societies. In 1981, an international survey asked respondents to rate how important God was in their lives on a scale from 1 (not important) to 10 (the highest importance). The score for Americans—8.21—was exceeded only by the score for South Africans. Other average scores among the fifteen nations studied were: Italy, 6.96; Great Britain, 5.72; West Germany, 5.67; France, 4.72; and Sweden, 3.99 (Gallup 1985:50).

The differences among these modern countries cannot be explained in terms of the broad historical processes so far discussed and need to be understood in terms of local historical and cultural circumstances. Moreover, rejection of 'God' may only mean rejection of a particular definition of this concept—not true atheism or agnosticism. Again, some nonbelievers may not be rejecting all religions, just ones built on belief in a supernatural world-creator. Overall, however, Gallup's data is consistent with the possibility that secularism has increased in the West.

In sum, secularism has become a larger part of Western civilization as a result of processes that are not likely to diminish in importance—growing knowledge of diverse religions, spreading familiarity with the scientific mentality, and a greater understanding of the results of social science research. Doubt exceeds denial, but both lessen the influence of religion.

Desacralization

When people respond to persons, experiences, and things in nonreligious terms, then daily life is desacralized.[1] Somewhat more poetically, Max Weber referred to the loss of the bewitched quality of daily life, the fact that in modern society everyday life does not have an immediate religious significance. That is to say, even among modern people not secularized, life is disenchanted.

It seems undeniable that the texture of daily life in modern society is less religious than life in other times. A few examples follow. In traditional times, dancing and singing—indeed all artistic forms—possessed a religious or magical quality (Day 1984:73, 78, 89). In 1984, the

Metropolitan Museum exhibited a collection of art by the Maori of New Zealand. After the works had been installed, a Maori delegation performed a ritual in the museum involving dancing and chanting "in order to propitiate the spirits of their carved ancestors and protect the spectators from the wrath of the art" (Levin 1984:109). It is difficult to imagine a modern, Western person even thinking about the possibility that art objects might somehow be a source of spiritual power.

Physical objects in the modern world are evaluated in terms of functional and aesthetic criteria. When people buy a house, they consider such factors as the size of the rooms, whether the roof leaks, whether the house looks pretty, and so on. In traditional societies, the way homes were built expressed religious beliefs. Houses might be oriented to the heavens, for example, with front doors facing east, expressing the belief that human society should be in harmony with a particular view of the natural order. In contrast, modern people think only about whether the house is in working order, is well-designed for their personal uses, and is attractive. Practical and aesthetic norms guide the many decisions we make about material objects.

Relatively recently, however, people interpreted unusual events as religious messages. The cholera epidemics in nineteenth-century Europe, for example, were explained by clergy as punishment from God (McLeod 1981:81). Similarly, a great train wreck in those days would be given religious meaning (Chadwick 1975:259). When a plane crashes today, we consult not oracles or priests but technical experts. Modern life is desacralized. Much that happens to us has no immediate religious significance.

This desacralization has resulted in part from the growth of technology. Recourse to religion is often related to experiences of insecurity and helplessness. When our lives are threatened or when we seem at the mercy of natural or social forces beyond our control, religious ideas and actions tend to capture our attention. However, technology has allowed humanity to lessen material scarcity and has given human beings an increased sense of collective and individual control over destiny. The material world is seen less as a locus of spiritual forces and more as a set of objects to be manipulated.

Antihumanitarian uses of scientific achievements (such as building nuclear bombs or polluting the environment) no doubt make some modern people feel helpless, and sometimes therefore religious. It cannot be denied that reasons exist for feeling helpless, even in modern societies, and that such feelings may motivate religiosity. On the other hand, technology has increased human control of the environment, and this has probably lessened the need for religious consolation and magical power in daily life. In modern society, nature has to a significant extent been despiritualized, making magicians mere entertainers and bringing about a world of powerful technocrats and scientists.

Feelings of helplessness have become less frequent not only because of technological development. A new welfare model of the state has been increasingly used by governments. This has given the poor, the handicapped, the sick, and others greater control over their lives.

Another factor responsible for desacralization concerns the way we think. In a sense, religion has become a separate compartment in our minds, with other compartments containing philosophy, physics, home economics, and so on. The first historian was the famous Athenian Thucydides, of the fourth century B.C. Before the period of classical Greek culture, representations of the past were a combination of history and religion, which we call myths. In modern society, history is used as often as religion (possibly even more often) to explain events. The varied academic departments of a modern university express the high degree of cultural differentiation and specialization which has resulted from the accumulation of knowledge and ideas in modern societies.

Especially significant is the differentiation of religion and ethics. In traditional societies, ethics was an aspect of religion. Historically, Christianity has played a critical role in the development of Western ethics. Ideas about human rights, for example, have Christian antecedents. However, even the doctrine of human rights now appears in secular garb (Stackhouse 1981:301). The United Nations Declaration on Human Rights does not support the claim that rights must be respected with reference to biblical or church sources. The English language has adjusted to the fact of cultural differentiation. The *Humanist* label has been created to identify a person who espouses a nonreligious, universalistic morality. About 60 percent of Americans agree that someone can be moral without believing in God (New York Times 1984b). Of course, not all modern people think of religion and ethics as separate from one another. The point is, however, that at the cultural level these intellectual disciplines have become differentiated, and they are thus available to people as distinct guides for making choices.

Desacralization, then, has resulted from the growth of technology, the appearance of the welfare state, and cultural differentiation. I want to be quite emphatic that I am not claiming that daily life is losing all religious significance. I am suggesting that daily life in the modern world usually has no immediate religious significance. It is only the unusual event that is filled with religious meaning—such is desacralization.

Structural Differentiation

Another aspect of the secularization thesis is that religious organizations have become less important in modern societies. Desacralization referred to the retreat of a religious perspective from daily life. Structural differentiation concerns the declining role of religious organizations.

According to modernization theory, social organizations have become more and more specialized. Historically, this means that activities or functions formerly performed by the occupants of familial or religious roles have become separated from these roles and are carried out by the occupants of new roles, roles that are not part of the family or a religious organization. Structural differentiation means the emergence of new organizations having primary responsibility for activities formerly performed by kin or religious specialists.

With regard to religion there are numerous examples. In the distant past, the care of the sick was a religious function, as suggested by the role of the Indian 'medicine man.' In European societies, education had been carried out solely by religious specialists such as monks and priests (and later by nuns). Today, there are secular schools. The modern welfare institution has also partially replaced churches in being responsible for the poor, the handicapped, and so on. The relatively new leisure and entertainment industries have lessened the social role of churches. As Wilson (1978:410) has noted: "The clergyman has relinquished many of his roles to the physician, the lawyer, the social worker, the teacher, and the psychiatrist"—and the television.

Of course, this is not to say that clergy are no longer involved in any of these differentiated activities. In the United States, faith healing is receiving new attention and religious schools are increasing. Religious groups such as the Salvation Army carry out important welfare work. The point is not that religious organizations have ceased to carry out such activities, but rather that numerous new types of organizations and roles (such as secular schools and the counselling profession) have come into existence. These new roles and organizations have lessened peoples' dependence on religious organizations for the satisfaction of needs and wants. It would seem, therefore, that over the course of Western history, religious organizations have lost power.

Privatization

Desacralization and structural differentiation have meant the creation of a religious neutral zone. When we select a chair because it is comfortable, or when we go to a medical doctor because we are sick, the subject of religion is usually considered simply irrelevant. In contrast, privatization concerns decisions regarding which religions claim relevancy. More specifically, it means that most modern people do not utilize religious beliefs and values when acting out their public roles.

Dividing life into public and private realms suggests that religion has little influence on the public institutions (i.e., the economic and political ones) but does influence private life (i.e., family life and leisure time activities). In this analysis, the religious institution is perceived as being shaped by economic and political forces—as forever accommodating to such forces rather than controlling them (Luckmann 1967). At the same time, it is allowed that religious values are "relevant for interpersonal relations, for face-to-face contacts, for the intimacies of the family, courtship, friendship, and neighborliness" (Wilson 1976:6).

Religious variables are more strongly correlated with attitudes associated with the private sphere, such as attitudes about sex and family life, than with other attitudes (Hoge 1979:105). People report that religion has greater influence on how they behave in family matters than on how they perform their jobs or on how they choose among candidates for political office (Tamney and Johnson 1985). These findings are consistent with the privatization thesis.

At present, it would seem that religious beliefs and values significantly affect family life and moderately influence other parts of the private sphere as well as interpersonal relations in the public institutions, but they are probably not importantly affecting key political and economic decisions. In attempting to explain privatization, we will first consider the relationship between religion and the economy, and then the relationship between religion and politics.

The development of modern economies has meant a loss of religious influence over work. In medieval Europe, there were two fundamental premises regarding the economy—"that economic interests are subordinate to the real business of life, which is salvation, and that economic conduct is one aspect of personal conduct, upon which, as on other parts of it, the rules of morality are binding" (Tawney 1947:34). The transformation of European economies into capitalistic systems meant that economic decisions were determined primarily by one motive, the desire for wealth.

The pursuit of profit is the pursuit of self-interest. Given that all religions emphasize the desirability of concern and sacrifice for others, religious values are often inconsistent with actions guided by the profit motive. The dominance of the latter means that religious values have little or no place in the modern economic system.

In 1937, Robert and Helen Lynd wrote the second of their two well-known studies of Middletown, a small city that supposedly illustrated the nature of the North American way of life. In Middletown, so-called economic laws were regarded as reflecting the natural order. It was believed that people work only because they have to, and they have to work because they want money and what it can buy. It was accepted that the pursuit of profit in a competitive environment made the United States great, and Middletowners didn't like anything that would curtail this process (Lynd and Lynd 1937:408–409, 418).

In a frequently referred-to chapter on 'the Middletown spirit', the Lynds discussed the tension between two sets of values—those associated with business success (e.g., forcefulness, enterprise, shrewdness, power), and "lovable" qualities (e.g., kindness, friendliness, considerateness). While the latter values supposedly dominated the private world, it was acceptable to subordinate such values to the drive for success in business life. For instance, misrepresentation in advertising, retailing, and securities exchanges were legitimated by the philosophy of *caveat emptor*—i.e., let the buyer beware. Departures from moral codes as part of doing business became "ritualized and conventionalized to enable customary practices to continue without too great a strain on the values which these practices undercut" (Lynd and Lynd 1937:424). Today 'heartless' business practices are more likely than ever to be questioned, but even today behavior unacceptable between friends is tolerated between people involved in a business deal.

A classic statement of American economic ideology appeared in the "Public Letter Box" of *The Muncie Star* (25 February 1974), the morning newspaper of the Lynd's Middletown.

Constructive Greed

"A Capitalist"

Wednesday's editorial commending Fredrick J. Thompson for his unselfishness in accepting a $6,930 suggestion award form Delco Battery demonstrates a common but serious misunderstanding of free enterprise economics.

The writer quoted Thompson as saying that "I'll keep suggesting as long as I am here because it helps all of us. Better ideas cut costs by saving time and materials."

The editorial went on to cite Thompson as "a man who understands economics and the free enterprise system" and praised him for his corporate responsibility.

I would prefer to think that Thompson was in it for the money, and by no means do I mean the observation as an insult. The essence of free enterprise is individualism, not corporate teamwork, and this is what won Thompson the award.

Preoccupation with the stance of one's employer beyond the point it affects his individual well-being is only a veiled form of socialism. By the same token, a worker who does less than he should is a defacto socialist by preying on the gullibility of the loyal.

Had I been Thompson I would have admitted I was after the money and complemented management for having the foresight to offer the award in the first place.

This letter from "a capitalist" was a classic expression of the "Middletown spirit": the primary motive for economic action is to increase personal wealth; one should think not of teamwork but individual advancement; anything beyond thinking of one's own welfare is socialism.

The American economic system, then, is based on the assumption that people act out of self-interest, and the self is narrowly defined in terms of the individual actor. The system tries to use this motivation for the common good. In the process, egotistic behavior is encouraged. Admittedly, just because the ideology of the economic sector assumes egoism does not mean that people are in fact always motivated by selfishness. Business people are sometimes concerned about social justice. The point is not that all Americans act selfishly in public life; rather, economic values and norms assume egoism, and this is not a cultural environment supportive of religious values.

These comments clearly refer to capitalist economies, particularly that of the United States. In democratic socialist countries, it may be true that religious and moral considerations do significantly influence the nature of economies. In the Western world, there are diverse economic systems which are more or less market-driven. Compared to premodern economies, however, all modern ones are to some extent capitalistic, and these economies tend to cultivate greed, envy, and materialism.

Bureaucratization of work has also contributed to privatization. With modernization, fewer and fewer people work for themselves; rather, they work in larger and larger organizations which tend to be bureaucratically organized. Illustrative of this process is the decline in the number of Americans living on farms. According to the U.S. Census Bureau, as recently as 1930 one American out of four lived on a farm. In 1985 the figure was one American in 45. The self-employed worker is becoming a rarity, replaced by someone who works for others in a job with predetermined duties and responsibilities. In short, workers have lost control of their lives to others and to bureaucratization. As a result, the values workers bring to their jobs, including religious values, have less relevance.

Privatization also means a lack of religious influence on political institutions. Although church-state relations vary among the countries of the world, the historical trend has been toward the separation of the government and religious organizations. As a result, religious leaders have played less and less of a direct political role in society. The current Iranian situation, in which final political authority rests with Islamic scholars, stands out because it is so unusual. The process of structural differentiation suggests that in the modern world religious organizations will not exercise political power. But the privatization of religion thesis implies more than this. It affirms that religious values have lost political significance.

Church-state separation has gone further in the United States than perhaps anywhere else, and antagonism toward political involvement of church leaders is probably stronger in this country than in any other outside the communist world. In a 1957 poll, Americans were asked: "Should the churches keep out of political matters—or should they express their views on day-to-day social and political questions?" The responses were: "keep out," 44 percent; "express views," 47 percent; and "no opinion," 9 percent (Gallup 1972:1480). Similar attitudes were found in 1968 (Gallup 1972:2120) and during the 1984 presidential election (Gallup 1985:11). To this day, Americans resist direct political involvement by religious organizations, and this restricts the influence religion can have in the public realm.

As stated earlier, Western countries differ in the extent to which state and church are separated. But in no Western country did an established church side with the popular struggle for political freedom. All three great Western revolutions—American, French, and Russian—included attempts to limit the political power of churches. The struggle for freedom in the West has pitted popular rebellions against state-church alliances. *Webster's New World Dictionary*, reflecting the historical association of the search for freedom and religious dissent, defines a *free-thinker* as "a person who forms his opinions about religion independently of tradition, authority, or established belief," and gives *atheist* as a synonym, suggesting that it is believed that free-thinking leads to the rejection of supernatural religion. The result is public opinion that tends not to favor political involvement by church groups, and this has contributed to the privatization of religion in the West.

Another explanation for the general privatization of religion is that it was encouraged at least indirectly by some religious leaders.The privatization thesis is not ahistorical. The division into private and public spheres is a product of our time and reflects not a universal theoretical perspective but an analysis of contemporary society. It was only during the last two centuries that the contemporary "distinction between public and private activities, or spheres of life, was sharpened...." (Bender 1978:114). It was the separation of workplace and home, and the elimination from the household of relative strangers (boarders) and paid labor (servants), that allowed the home to be experienced as a private place and the private family to become an ideal. In colonial times, there was much legal regulation of the family. Spouses, for example, were fined for using "ill words" (Laslett 1973:487). During the last century, however, it came to be accepted that family life is a private matter, which implies that a family should have a high degree of self-determination or self-control. Thus, in the last century the family came to be seen as a distinct, almost self-contained, part of life.

Concomitant with this change, many nineteenth-century clergy idealized the family. There was a body of religious literature that portrayed the new industrial enterprises and the cities as evil. Writers and preachers of such images came to think of the home as a haven and sanctuary against the evils of industrial jobs and big city temptations. It was thought, or at least hoped, that with diligent effort "the family could actually become a heaven on earth" (Jeffrey 1972:22). Thus, in the last century, and especially among the clergy bent on moral reform rather than social change, religion became closely identified with family life. It was thought that religion could only have influence in the home, that the home was the only place where traditional morality could be preserved and practiced. Clergy who thought this way did not try to increase the political significance of their religious world view.

There are reasons, then, for accepting the privatization thesis— the nature of modern economies, a popular distrust of church-state entanglement, and a focus by some religious leaders on the home as the only place where religion can matter.

Christian Commitment

The discussion of secularization has established that in modern milieus there is an increased likelihood of secularism and religious doubt, desacralization, a weakened church role, and privatization. Except in the case of outright secularism, none of these changes means that individuals have ceased to care about religion. I will now consider the relation between modernization and personal religious commitment. In the following discussion, the distinction between commitment to Christ and commitment to a church will not be made. Although the latter has been more negatively affected by modernization, both forms of commitment have had parallel histories.

No one can prove whether religious commitment has changed since the days of the Greek city-states, or whether such commitment in the present century is significantly different from what prevailed before industrialization. The needed information does not exist. It is even difficult to find agreement about changes in religious commitment over the past half-century. Although relevant information exists for these years, there is no agreed-upon measure of religious commitment. What is clear, however, is that since the Middle Ages there have been significant criticisms of Christianity, criticisms which indicate the presence of alienation from existing churches, and these criticisms have not been random. They have demonstrated the existence of ideological opposition to Christianity and a lack of personal commitment to this religion.

As the Dark Ages faded away, there reemerged in Western Europe an interest in and commitment to the value of the individual. This liberal revolution had its roots in the Hebrew prophets, Greek philosophers, and Athenian democracy, as well as in the Sermon on the Mount. The valuing of freedom accelerated with the collapse of medieval Europe. Between 1100 and 1800, such libertarian notions as individual freedom and the dignity of the individual person were elaborated on and became powerful political forces in Western history.

The religious significance of libertarian ideas can be seen in the history of Protestantism. Of course, the very existence of Protestantism is due in part to the power of libertarianism. Likewise, the almost continuous fragmentation of Protestantism has been due in part to attempts to make churches more and more libertarian.

The Protestant Reformation involved a religious form of individualism. This is expressed in Luther's doctrine of the priesthood of all believers. Although Luther's religion was quite conservative, it did stress the individual in relation to God, and thus his religion began the process of undermining religious authoritarianism. Calvinism furthered this process. There is "an inward affinity" between democracy and Calvinism (Troeltsch 1931:640). Both give great importance to the individual: "The Calvinist is filled with a deep sense of a Divine mission to the world, of being mercifully privileged among thousands, and in possession of an immeasurable responsibility" (Troeltsch 1931:617). Yet Calvinists combined this religious individualism "with a strong bias towards authority and a sense of the unchangeable nature of law" (Troeltsch 1931:619).

During the English Revolution (1640–1660), new religions such as Quakerism were formed which embodied libertarian values more than the established churches. At that time in English history, "the critique of the established church was so radically anticlerical as to be virtually secularist in content" (Hill 1986:195–196). Two processes were going on at the same time. First, an awareness of diverse religions and the popularization of science were feeding a growing secularism. And second, ideas about individual rights found expression in new, more democratic churches such as the Society of Friends (the Quakers) and the Baptist churches.

Over the past several hundred years, then, the Christian religion has been adjusting to the appearance and appeal of the libertarian ideational set. The continuing subdividing of Christianity, culminating in churches such as Unitarian-Universalism, was at least in part an expression of religious discontent generated by a commitment to libertarian ideals. This process is not over, as is revealed in the recent history of the Catholic church which I shall discuss. The rise of libertarianism, then, is the first modern cultural crisis that challenged commitment to Christianity. Over the centuries, however, Christianity has adjusted to liberal ideas, thus minimizing any negative impact they might have had on the religious institution in the West.

Another crisis accompanied the growth of industrialization. McLeod (1981) has analyzed the course of religion in Western Europe during the years 1784 to 1970, which he believed was a distinct historical period for this civilization. After reviewing relevant historical studies, he concluded that the period was marked by widespread revolt against the churches (McLeod 1981:V). The most significant aspect of this second crisis was the alienation of the working class, which had crystalized as a self-conscious part of society. Christianity has taken on many forms, of course, and in recent European history some of these forms have attracted strong worker commitment either because a church was a vehicle for the political struggle for freedom (the Lutheran church in World War II Norway) or because of the fusion of religion and ethnicity (Ireland). But by and large, as the working class formed and developed, Christianity was perceived as anti-worker. The poor, finding that clergy sided with the economic elite, simply gave up attending services. Alienation of the working class was furthered by the appearance of socialist and anarchist ideologies which tried to define and explain working class issues and which were at times antichurch (McLeod 1981:71).

This alienation of the working class from the churches also occurred in the United States during industrialization. Samuel Gompers, then-President of the A F of L, told Francis Perry: "My associates have come to look upon the church and the ministry as the apologists and defenders of the wrong committed against the interests of the people...." (1899:622) As the twentieth century began, many American workers were alienated from the churches, and indeed from religion. As shall be discussed in Part I of this book, Christianity is still trying to contain the crisis started by the industrial revolution and expressed most forcefully in the writings of socialist critics of industrial society.

In the 1960s, a different crisis became clear in the Western world. Across Europe and in the United States, there has been a decline in church attendance for Christianity as a whole (McLeod 1981:134–135; Chaves 1989). This has been accompanied by an increase in the percentage of the population not claiming any religious affiliation (Condran and Tamney 1985). During the seventies and eighties, measures of countercultural involvement have been found to be related to weakness of religious commitment, not attending church, and having no religious affiliation (Perrin 1989; Tamney, Powell, and Johnson 1989).

Consistent with this analysis, research has indicated that, prior to 1960, the religiously alienated came disproportionately from the working class, but after 1960 religious alienation has increased among the upper classes (Condran and Tamney 1985; Roozen 1980:437). Thus, in the United States and elsewhere, the nature of the religious crisis seems to have changed from being related to socialist values to being primarily the result of religious conflict with countercultural values.

Another important development in the sixties was related to gender roles. The movement to liberate women has had religious implications. There is both a structural and a cultural aspect to the negative attitudes of liberated women toward existing religions as they reject both sexual discrimination practices of churches and religious imagery and theology that supports a traditional role for women in society. The women's liberation movement has had religious consequences ranging from calls to reorganize Christian churches to attempts at creating new religions. In fact, women holding a liberated attitude are more likely than other women to have no religious affiliation (Condran and Tamney 1985). The women's movement, then, is a second aspect to the crisis that began in the 1960s.

The crises just reviewed can be examined in terms of social groups. The history of Christianity in the modern period can be organized in terms of the difficulties churches have had in gaining the commitment of the bourgeoisie, the working class, the liberally educated, and women. However, the beliefs and values historically associated with a specific group do not remain the exclusive province of that group. Thus, the emphasis is placed on new values rather than on newly formed social groups.

The issue of religious commitment, therefore, will be analyzed in terms of Christianity's need to adjust to the Western values historically associated with the aforementioned social groups. (The values and beliefs to be discussed may universally accompany modernization, but this is debatable, and the issue is beyond the scope of this book.) These ideational sets are secular in the sense that, for the most part, they have been developed and championed by individuals and organizations not specifically religious. Four such sets have appeared during modernization: the libertarian, the socialist, the countercultural, and the feminist. During the course of modernization, churches have lost the commitment of people who have espoused these ideational sets because the churches were authoritarian and male-dominated, sided with the upper class, and attacked countercultural values. In general, however, Christianity has adjusted to the libertarian set more than to the others. The contemporary lack of religious commitment in the West is the result of a continuing conflict between Christianity and all four ideational sets. None of the crises described has been completely resolved, although in different countries the importance of each crisis varies.

Summary: Modernization and Secularization

Modernization can be described in terms of several sets of traits, some of which seem unlikely to be rejected or abandoned without a nuclear war, invasion from outer space, or other such catastrophe. First are the universal and relatively irreversible aspects of modernization: technological growth, scientific development, structural differentiation, cultural pluralism, cultural differentiation, and the secular ideational sets (libertarian, socialist, countercultural, and feminist). Second are those traits which, currently widespread in Western civilization, may not be permanent features of a modernized society: a profit-oriented and bureaucratized economy, the welfare state, public opposition to political involvement of religious leaders, and the preference of some religious leaders to focus mainly on the private realm. This analysis of modernity is from the point of view of someone interested in secularization; other perspectives would produce related but different constructions of modernity.

Modernization is producing secularization. Following is a brief summary of the facets of this process.

1. Secularism seems to have increased as a result of awareness of cultural pluralism, the scientific attitude, and social scientific findings relating to religion.

2. Desacralization has increased because of technological growth, the acceptance of the welfare state, and cultural differentiation.

3. Structural differentiation has meant a weakened role for religious organizations. In contemporary society, religious organizations serve fewer needs of people than ever before.

4. Christianity is privatized; it has little influence in the public realm. This fact has resulted from the nature of modern economies, the existence of a public that distrusts the political involvement of clergy, and the preference of some religious leaders to be concerned only with the private realm.

5. Commitment to Christianity has been limited by the failure of Christianity to adjust to modern ideas which have expressed the needs and aspirations of the bourgeoisie, the working class, educated people, and women.

Secularization, then, means secularism, desacralization, weakened religious organizations, privatization, and a lack of religious commitment. Table 1 summarizes the argument about the relationship between modernization and secularization. The likely permanence of some characteristics of a modern society would seem to ensure a lessened role for religion in contemporary society. Secularism, desacralization, and a weakened role for religious organizations seem to be permanent features of a modern society. This is not to say that every modern person will soon be an atheist, never think about religion, and never visit a church or consult the clergy. These are relative matters. For example, it is expected only that secularism will be more prevalent in the future than in the past, not that everyone will eventually be a secularist. It should be noted that one aspect of Table 1 may be misleading. Although it is indicated that the failure of Christianity to adjust to modern ideas such as libertarian ones is reversible, at the same time it needs to be clear that the existence of such ideas is considered an irreversible aspect of modernization.

TABLE 1

Summary of Modernization-Secularization Analysis

Secularization Aspect	Causes	Reversible
Secularism	Religious Pluralism Scientific Attitude Social Science Research	
Desacralization	Technological Growth Cultural Differentiation Welfare State	 x
Weakened Church Role	Structural Differentiation	

Privatization	Modern Economy
	Public Opinion on the
	    Political Involvement of Clergy
	Religious Preference for
	    Private Realm
		x
		
		x
		
		x

Weakened Commitment to Christianity	Failure to adjust to: -libertarian ideas -socialist ideas -countercultural ideas -feminist ideas	 x x x x

While some aspects of secularization seem to be here to stay, others—notably, privatization and the lessened commitment to Christianity—are quite open to change. Modern traits such as a capitalist economy and public opposition to mixing religion and politics seem relatively impermanent. Moreover, Christianity has been trying to adjust to modern ideas, as shall be discussed in detail. So the ultimate fate of religion in a modern society is an open question.

Of course, the relative irreversibility of some components of secularization limits the extent of possible change regarding Christian commitment and privatization. That is to say, if such things as secularism do increase, then any increase in Christian commitment and influence is necessarily limited. In other words, although most of the factors specifically affecting privatization and Christian commitment are reversible, this possibility must be understood in the context of seemingly irreversible increases in other aspects of secularization.

The Religious Response to Secularization

Nothing in the preceding arguments implies that churches must simply accept the present situation, and indeed they have not. A remarkable feature of recent times is that churches and individuals have increasingly taken up the challenge presented by secularization. Such action, of course, becomes part of the secularization process and will affect its course. Modernization is limiting religious popularity, but the degree of limitation depends in part on the reaction of religion to modernization.

Broadly speaking, there are two types of response to modernization and its consequences. Some religions adapt to modernization. They accept the irreversible aspects of this process and their religious consequences, while they seek to reverse the changeable aspects of modernization. These are the liberal religions. Other religions, the traditionalist ones, struggle against secularization in all its forms. The existence of these alternative responses raises some obvious questions. How much accommodation by liberal religion is feasible? What is the fate of religions that seem to be swimming against the tide? Such matters will be considered in the following discussion.

Religious popularity, however, is not simply a result of modernization and the religious response to it. The discussion of the relationship between modernization and religion, therefore, needs to be based on a general theory of religious popularity.[2]

A Theoretical Framework for the Analysis of Religious Popularity

Only the situation of modernizing, or modern, societies will be considered. The following four propositions will serve as an initial explanation of religious popularity.

Proposition 1: A religion will be more popular to the extent that it is compatible with modernity.   People will find a religion appealing to the extent that it fits their social conditions. When a religion does not ask people to give up or destroy what they have found to be unavoidable or useful, it is more likely to be popular. For instance, in a modern situation it is difficult to live unaware of cultural diversity; the option of fruitlessly condemning this diversity is less satisfying than learning to live with it.

In the following discussion, emphasis is given to the cultural side of modernization and to the modern ideational sets in particular; therefore, some elaboration on the meaning of these sets is appropriate. The libertarian set developed along with modernization, emphasizing the values of individual freedom and dignity, especially in relation to the state. This ideational set focuses on political liberties, popular sovereignty, and rational persuasion as a means of gaining compliance with social norms. The word *socialism* refers to a core of ideas that arose in reaction to industrialization with its accompanying social inequalities and sometimes ruthless competition. Ideals such as solidarity, economic cooperation, and social justice became collectively identified as socialism. Socialists, therefore, have been especially interested in the economic institution and the idea of economic rights such as the right to work. The counterculture focuses on self-development as well as self-satisfaction and relates especially to the so-called private realm. Feminism, in part, involves the application of the other ideational sets to the particular situation of women and, in part, challenges masculine values such as dominance and mastery. A central theme of this work is the absence of religious popularity in the West as a result of the failure of Christianity to sufficiently accommodate these modern ideas.

Proposition 2: A religion will be more popular to the extent that it is supported by the state. With modernization the state has emerged as a powerful, autonomous institution. The state typically controls or influences agencies of socialization such as schools and the mass media through laws, funding, and censorship. A state cannot remain completely neutral toward values. Whether explicitly in a constitution or implicitly in a tradition, each state identifies with certain values; thus, the state can never be completely neutral toward all values, and its actions will influence the appeal of religions. The inevitability of the state's need for a platform of values led Rousseau (1974) to argue that, in the absence of a common religion, a government would create a "civil religion."

Proposition 3: A religion will be more popular the greater the breadth of needs served by the social organizational carrier of the religion. Not all religions are supported by a social organization in all places. If a religious organization does exist, people can be attracted by the feeling of solidarity at religious meetings, possibly by the prestige of being a church member, by the advice of comrades about jobs, and so on.

Proposition 4: A religion will be more popular to the extent that it is part of ethnic and national identities. Individuals commonly identify themselves (at least in part) in terms of their membership in groups.

The most pervasive examples are thinking of oneself as a member of a family or ethnic group or, in modern times, a nationality. Identifying with such groups seems to anchor personal identity. Because the following analysis is at the macro level, the aforementioned proposition refers to ethnic and national identities only. Given the tendency for people to define themselves in terms of group affiliation, if a religion is part of a specific ethnic or national identity, it will be more popular among those who compose the corresponding groups.

Although it is assumed, for now, that the factors in these propositions are the main determinants of religious popularity, they are not the only relevant forces. Undoubtedly, in the short run the popularity of a religion is dependent on the resources of its supporters, such as their money and skills (McCarthy and Zald 1977). It is assumed, however, that in the long run resources are influenced by the aforementioned four factors. Therefore, not much attention will be given to detailing the resources of social movements. Moreover, the four propositions do not take demographic factors into consideration. The popularity of a religion in a particular time and place is related to such things as the birth and death rates of its adherents. For example, liberal religions are declining in the United States in part because their members have relatively few children (Roof and McKinney 1987:161). Finally, there are changes that occur as any religion is elaborated that sometimes result in schisms. Sociologists have argued that, with time, religious groups experience rationalization, with negative consequences for popularity. In theory, religious thought becomes more rational in the formal sense of becoming more systematic and internally consistent and more rational in the substantive sense of eliminating fantasy and mythic elements (O'Dea 1966:44). It is argued that such changes create discontent, which results in protest movements, some of which become new religions. However, schisms may actually increase the overall popularity of a religion such as Christianity. In any case, this work does not claim to consider all the factors relevant to explaining religious popularity; it is suggested, however, that what is discussed are factors crucial to the long-term popularity of a religion in a modern society.[3]

Plan of the Book

The point is to explore the usefulness of my theoretical framework for understanding the appeal of Christianity in the modern world. Because it is assumed that the first proposition is the most important of the four, and because it seems that the absence of popularity in recent centuries is the result of Christianity's failure to adapt to the modern ideational sets, this work focuses on the relation between this religion and these modern ideas. Part I considers the relationship between Christianity and socialist ideas. Part II concerns this religion and the counterculture.

These abstract issues are considered using significant case studies. Regarding religion and socialism, two situations are analyzed. Chapter 1 considers how the Catholic church responded to the Solidarity movement in Poland, and Chapter 2 examines the response of this church to the Liberation Theology movement in Latin America. Why do I use these particular case studies? The confrontation between Christianity and socialist ideas is greatest in Latin America and Eastern Europe, and Liberation Theology and Solidarity are the two most popular expressions of support for socialist ideas in these regions.

In considering the relationship between religion and the counterculture, one case illustrates an accommodative response while another is an example of a traditionalist reaction. Chapter 4 is a discussion of how American Protestantism has adapted to the counterculture. However, a part of Protestantism, the Christian Right, has seemingly refused to make such an accommodation. Chapter 5 examines why, contrary to the theory, such a religion prospers in a modern society. In the course of analyzing all four case studies, mention will be made of religious responses to libertarianism as well as to the ideas expressed in Propositions 2, 3, and 4. Because a consideration of feminism is beyond my expertise, the relationship between religion and feminist ideas will not be discussed.

The case studies are used to test and develop the rather simple theoretical framework just presented. Of particular interest is whether there are limits to how much religion will accommodate modernity. The conclusion presents a more sophisticated framework for the analysis of religious popularity and uses it to discuss the resilience of Christianity in the modern world.

Part I

Christianity and Socialism

❖ ——————————————————— ❖

Catholicism and the
Solidarity Movement
in Poland

During the past two centuries, many members of the lower class have remained indifferent or hostile to the churches because these religious organizations failed to sympathize with movements seeking to improve the lot of laborers of all kinds. It is equally true that, during the present century, Christian churches have changed in the direction of supporting working-class causes. In this and the following chapter, the focus is on Roman Catholicism, but the basic issue is the analysis of the process of the accommodation of liberal Christianity to new social forces resulting from industrialization. The needs of the working class were expressed in the aspirations of socialism, and gradually the Catholic church has adapted itself to the existence of this new class and to the socialist ideals espoused by the champions of this class.

This chapter considers the situation in Poland during the 1980s, when the Solidarity movement was engaged in a political struggle with the Communist government. The question is: What role was played by the Polish Catholic church at this time? The main concern of this chapter is the interaction between the Catholic church in Poland and the Solidarity social movement, which spoke for the working class. What actually happens when the church must interact with a socialist movement?

In the course of the analysis, it will be shown that the popularity of Polish Catholicism, in spite of secularization, can be understood using the theoretical framework just presented. But the more important goal of this chapter is to extend the theoretical framework by asking whether there are limits to the extent Catholicism will accommodate socialism.

To begin with, however, relevant changes in Catholic church social teaching will be briefly described. Then, the Polish situation will be analyzed.

Roman Catholic Social Teaching

Prior to the present century, Catholic theology was dominated by a medieval world view that valued social obligations over individual rights. Medieval thought, including the work of Thomas Aquinas, did not include a theory of human rights. Even at the time of Leo XIII (1878–1903), within official Catholic circles individual freedom was considered subversive, and the masses were believed to be in need of guidance in all spheres of life. Differences in power were viewed as the natural result of inequalities in abilities. All classes and groups were supposedly equally obliged to work for the common good; social conflict was seen as unnatural and destructive to all parties involved (Curran 1985).

This world view started to change when the European working class began to be tempted by Marxist ideas and to abandon the church. In response, a series of papal encyclicals (beginning with *Rerum Novarum* in 1891) appeared that sympathetically analyzed the plight of workers. Despite some innovation, certain basic ideas from the past were retained, notably the acceptance of private property and the rejection of class struggle (Pawlikowski 1986).

Although the defense of private property has been a basic Catholic doctrine, since Vatican II even the right to private property has been viewed differently. In the documents of this council, the most basic principle concerning property is that all goods exist to serve the needs of all. As a consequence, the right to private property is subordinated to everyone's "right to a share of earthly goods sufficient to oneself and one's family" (Curran 1985:27).

Concurrently, the church's attitude toward socialism, even Marxism, has become more open. Marxism as a complete ideology is condemned, but a Marxist social analysis is considered potentially useful. Current Catholic thought about the economy is contained in the encyclical *Laborem Exercens*, published in 1981. It was written by Pope John Paul II, who grew up and worked almost all his life in Poland.

Laborem Exercens

The pope's letter emphasizes the centrality of work for humanity and the psychological needs of the individual worker. We are warned that, at times, modern technology "reduces man to the status of its slave" (John Paul II 1984:280). Then the pope makes his basic point, that jobs may differ in their objective value (i.e., the worth of their contributions to society), but all jobs must contribute to the self-realization of workers' human nature. A brief summary of the encyclical follows.

The error of early capitalism was to treat workers as just another factor of production—like machinery. Section Three of the encyclical is titled "The Priority of Labor Over Capital," but this priority does not imply any necessary conflict. Recent industrial strife has occurred because those involved failed to properly order their goals. The productive process will be moral and peaceful if it is based on "the principle of the substantial and real priority of labor...independent of the nature of the services provided by the worker" (290).

The pope differentiated church doctrine from "the program of collectivism as proclaimed by Marxism" and "the program of capitalism practiced by liberalism" (292). The church upholds the right of private ownership, but "the right to private property is subordinated to the right to common use, to the fact that goods are meant for everyone" (293). Moreover, the state is responsible for developing an economic plan that ensures suitable employment for all. In certain circumstances, not specified in the essay, nationalization may be justified. The "position of 'rigid' capitalism continues to remain unacceptable, namely the position that defends the exclusive right to private ownership of the means of production as an untouchable 'dogma' of economic life" (293). This may mean not only the occasional nationalization of a segment of the economy, but also joint ownership by workers and management, profit-sharing, and worker participation in management. In all such matters, workers must be able to believe they are working for themselves (294–295).

Nation-states, without losing their sovereignty, must work together to produce a just world economy. The pope criticized transnational corporations whose policies increase the economic gap between rich and poor nations and who, by forcing producers in poor countries to sell their goods cheaply, contribute to the existence of inhumane working conditions in the third world.

Fundamentally, work is a means of building community. Unions have a right to fight for workers' rights, but "union demands cannot be turned into a kind of group or class 'egoism,' although they can and should also aim at correcting—with a view to the common good of the whole of society—everything defective in the system of ownership of the means of production or in the way these are managed" (302).

As this encyclical illustrates, Catholicism has changed in the direction of accommodating socialist values and goals. However, it is insufficient to consider only abstract ideas. Religious and secular ideologies are embedded in specific groups. Thus, we need to know how the church and socialist movements relate to each other. Two such movements are considered—Solidarity and Liberation Theology—because the Catholic church has reacted differently to each of these movements. To begin with, how did the Polish Catholic church interact with Solidarity?

The remainder of this chapter will consider the following topics: (1) the religious situation in Poland; (2) the nature of the Solidarity movement; (3) how Solidarity related to the Catholic church; (4) how the church responded to Solidarity, and (5) recent post-Communism developments in Poland.

The Religious Situation

Popular support for the Catholic church seemed quite strong during the eighties (Piwowarski 1984:25). Churches were full, and many Poles spoke out in defense of the church. The church estimated that about 94 percent of Poles were Catholic, at least in the sense of having been baptized in the church (Zdaniewicz 1983:17). However, this popular appeal existed in spite of the occurrence of secularization. Religious studies of the Polish population have reported results consistent with the modernization-secularization thesis. First, the fact of secularization will be established. Second, the reasons for the church's popularity in a secularizing society will be discussed.

Secularization in Poland

In 1980, a national survey categorized the Polish population as follows: 54 percent were believers who attended religious services, 39 percent were believers who did not attend such services, and 7 percent were nonbelievers (Kostecki 1985:11). An official poll of Communist party members, the results of which were revealed in the underground press, found that 25 percent of them were believers and practicing Catholics, 49 percent were believers but seldom or never went to mass, and 14 percent were nonbelievers (Ascherson 1985:7). Thus, although only a minority of Poles reject Catholicism outright, a significant number seem only tenuously related to the church.

As elsewhere in the Western world, religiosity is higher among the less-educated, rural dwellers, women, and older people (Podgorecki 1976). For instance, a national study found that 55 percent of educated people (i.e., those with at least a high school education) were believers, compared with 97 percent of those who had no primary education (Darczewska 1983:68–69).

Religion remains more important in the lives of rural people, but even in rural areas things are changing. Magic has declined: "The practice of feeding sick livestock with blessed herbs has...significantly decreased." And signs of secularization exist among the rural people: "The customary greeting of Polish peasants, 'Blessed by Jesus Christ,' is giving way more and more to a secular 'Good Day' after the manner of the townspeople" (Chrypinski 1975:243).

Modernization has meant the emergence of "selective religiosity" (Marianski 1981:73). That is to say, Catholics are no longer accepting church pronouncements *en masse*; rather, individual Catholics are judging each edict and selecting which ones are worthy of obedience. This is especially true among urban, educated Poles. Polish priest and sociologist Wladyslaw Piwowarski (1984:31) estimated that only one-third of believers are fully orthodox Catholics, and an even smaller percentage are committed to all church moral teachings. "What is more, Catholics have begun to think of moral principles as something independent of religion" (Piwowarski 1976:319).

Secularism, desacralization, and "selective Catholicism" (a sign of weakening commitment) are increasing. There is a "narrowing of the range of questions associated with religion, motivated by religion, or valued from the viewpoint of religious norms," especially for matters concerning public life (Kubiak 1972:167). In other words, in Poland there is a privatization of theology. I want to make the point that, even in a country where religion seems so important as in Poland, modernization is producing secularization.[1]

Reasons for the Popularity of Catholicism in Secularized Poland

In the period under consideration, four points were important: (1) the church was closely associated with the national identity; 2) the church had an important political role in a totalitarian situation; (3) state action both limited and strengthened the church; and (4) the church developed a social doctrine that reflected the needs and aspirations of the working class. The first three points will be briefly discussed, and the remainder of this chapter will analyze the relationship between the church and the Solidarity movement.

To understand the strong connection between the Polish nation and Catholicism, one need not go back further than the last century. Between 1795 and 1918, there was no Polish state. What had been Poland had been divided among the Prussian, Russian, and Austrian empires. During this time, Polish culture was nurtured by the church. Only the Austrian regime was tolerant of Polish culture. Religious leaders opposed deliberate attempts at the germanization and russification of different segments of the Polish people. For example: "In

1874, the archbishop of Poznan...was imprisoned for opposing the introduction of German into religious instruction" (Civic 1983:93).

This bonding of nationalism and Catholicism that resulted from the church's assumption of the role of cultural protector was strengthened by the dissemination of a messianic view of Polish Catholicism by romantic intellectuals of the nineteenth century. "Briefly stated, the messianic view suggests that the Polish nation is the 'chosen people' of the New Covenant and is destined, through its suffering and constant martyrdom, to lead the nations of the world to salvation" (Pomian-Srzednicki 1982:38–39; for further discussion, *see* Morawska 1984). The church officially disapproves of this messianism, but some clergy have espoused this vision, and certainly messianic symbolism remains a part of Polish Catholicism.

At Easter, it is customary for Poles to visit a simulation or symbol of Christ's grave in a local church.

> Those who visited the grave in the Jesuit Church in the Old Town of Warsaw in 1978 found themselves confronted not with the dead Christ...but with a dead Poland symbolized by the Polish red and white standard pierced by two swords and surrounded by barbed wire.... The message on the standard read as follows: "And we too will rise again...." The sign of the cross was duly made by all those who filed past (Pomian-Srzednicki 1982:194).

Such ritual scenes had occurred during the last century (Morawska 1984:31).

The extent to which Polish messianism is accepted is not known, but a nationalistic church was legitimated by Cardinal Wyszinski who, until his recent death, was head of the Polish Catholic church.

> For us, next to God, our first love is Poland. After God one must above all remain faithful to the Homeland, to the Polish national culture. We will love all the people in the world, but only in such an order of priorities (Szajkowski 1983:V).

At a time when the Polish people felt captured by the Soviet Union, such a pronouncement must have evoked deep feelings of identification with the cardinal and the church.

A second factor enhancing the importance of the church was that it was *the* alternative institution to the party in Poland. A public opinion poll, conducted unofficially in Poland by a French agency shortly before John Paul II's visit in the summer of 1983, asked who best represented the interests of Polish society. Three percent of poles questioned said the party and government did, 24 percent said the illegal Solidarity, and 60 percent said the church and the pope (Morawska 1984:32).

The church was the locus and scaffolding for an alternative society. Bishops at times acted like union leaders, for example—protesting to the government about safety in the coal mines—and priests acted as legal advisors (Solidarity 1984:42–43). The church became the womb within which artists of various kinds were able to develop and display their works (Uncensored Poland 1985b). An important museum was the Museum of the Archdiocese of Warsaw, in which were displayed contemporary works that were quite expressive and relevant.

In Poland, the Communist party in fact controlled the various nominally independent institutions of society—the mass media, unions, and professional associations. In effect, structural differentiation did not exist. Dissidents of all kinds sought refuge in the church. Moreover, people turned to the clergy for a variety of services formally dominated by party affiliates. Poland had become almost two societies, the party and the church.

The third factor influencing the social role of the church was government policy, which was an expression of Communist party ideology. The Polish Communist party assumed that there would be a long and unavoidable ideological struggle with Catholicism (Loranc 1986). The government organized its own Catholic groups that supported the party, waged a propaganda campaign as part of "planned secularization," and established secular rituals (e.g., secular weddings, name-giving ceremonies, and funerals) (Pomian-Srzednicki 1982:68). Even the calendar was changed: "The year 1981 A.D. is no longer A.D., but O.E. signifying our era...." (Pomian-Srzednicki 1982:84). The state was rewriting history in a manner that identified Poland with the masses and the church hierarchy with foreign influence (Pomian-Srzednicki 1982:89). Religious instruction in the public schools was eliminated (Civic 1983:95–98). Moreover, in 1986 the state introduced religion classes in the high schools which the church believed were intended to foster atheism (Kaufman 1986b).

However, the party also had a short-term strategy regarding Catholicism that sought to take advantage of loyalty to the church (Loranc 1986). Concessions to the church were meant to neutralize it in the political arena and to weaken Solidarity. The government softened its repressive control of the Catholic church, for instance, by allowing the church to begin publishing long closed-down newspapers and magazines (Kozkowski 1987). In Machiavellian fashion, the government preferred to deal with the more conservative church rather than with Solidarity, both of which organizations were seeking to speak for the masses. This short-term strategy strengthened the church.

In sum, the Catholic church was popular during the eighties for three reasons: there was a close association of religion and national identity; in the totalitarian Polish state, the church became an alternative society performing a variety of social functions; and the party's short-term strategy enhanced the power of the church. The social role of the church made religious indifferentism unlikely. A Polish friend revealed the nature of the situation in this anecdote. When her adolescent stepdaughter mentioned that she was dating a young man who was an altar boy, the mother kidded her: Why was she going out with someone who must be a wimp, and not a fellow student who was a leader and in the avant-garde? Her child responded that her boyfriend was in fact a leader. At a time when priests were national martyrs, would-be heroes were altar boys.

A fourth reason for the church's popularity was the sympathy expressed for the workers' cause in the new social doctrine. But what happens when the church is faced with another organization that also espouses this cause? The remainder of this chapter concerns the interaction between the church and Solidarity, although the government cannot be ignored in the analysis. The purpose is to determine if there are limits to how much the church will accommodate a socialist program. To begin with, what was the Solidarity movement?

Solidarity

Solidarity was a social movement centered on a trade-union base that primarily sought to improve the life of the Polish working class, but it also struggled for national liberation and the democratization of society. Solidarity in the crystalized form of a trade union organization was declared illegal by the Polish government in 1981 but was given legal status again in 1989. The success of Solidarity was possible because of the failure of the Communist party. "According to a party-commissioned poll in 1976, only one in every five industrial workers thought that the party represented their interests" (Pravda 1983:79). In June 1981, Solidarity won 92 of the 100 seats to the Senate and 160 of the 161 seats to a lower house that it had been permitted to contest under the election rules (Tagliabue 1989c).

As a workers' movement, Solidarity fought for trade unions free from government control, better pay and pensions, longer maternity leaves, and the like. Moreover, Solidarity wanted to institutionalize the involvement of workers in making basic national, regional, and local economic policies, including investment and price policies (see the famous Gdansk Agreement of 1980 between Solidarity and the government in Brumberg 1983).

In 1981, the *Network of Solidarity Organizations in Leading Factories*, a branch of the Solidarity movement, dedicated itself to the goal of workers' self-management—to the "socialization" rather than the nationalization of the means of production. A socialized enterprise would be the communal property of all employees, and it would be run by a democratically elected workers' council, which would appoint a manager to direct the enterprise (Solidarity 1982a:178–179).

The goal of self-management must be understood in the context of the need for economic rationality. Self-management of enterprises was sought in order to free managers from the *nomenklatura* process—i.e., the appointment of people with politically correct ideas to key positions in all areas of public life, which workers believed had resulted in poor economic policies (Touraine et al. 1983:35). This negative goal was widely supported. There was disagreement, however, on what should determine economic decisions. Specifically, the workers disagreed on the extent to which managerial decisions should be governed by the market or by the workers themselves. In general, Solidarity tried to increase the power of workers while accepting that managers must have some independence, enabling them to act for purely long-term economic reasons (Touraine et al. 1983:94–95, 102).

Was Solidarity a socialist movement? On the basis of discussions with Polish workers, Touraine and his colleagues (1983:18, 50, 148) concluded that some workers favored capitalism, all wanted greater economic rationality, and most accepted socialism. A Solidarity advisor summed up the situation as follows: Solidarity sought socialist goals (i.e., greater worker control and the minimization of social and economic inequality) but rejected the classical socialist means to these goals (i.e., state ownership and completely centralized planning) and thus avoided the use of the socialist label (Geremek 1982:328). Solidarity was never united about needed economic reforms (Wolnicki 1989).

Solidarity's social model was based on the goals of social differentiation and political pluralism. The Gdansk Agreement included commitment to pluralistic mass media and full liberty of expression in public and professional life. The movement sought to create independent unions, a peasant organization, and an independent mass media—as well as to strengthen the Roman Catholic church by gaining it access to the media. Such goals as free elections, a free mass media, the achievement of civil liberties, and the creation of politically independent organizations such as unions all express what I have called the libertarian ideational set.

In addition to acting as a union, Solidarity was a nationalist movement "in the tradition of the uprisings of the eighteenth and nineteenth centuries and the Warsaw Rising of 1944" (Touraine et al. 1983:2). The Polish government was perceived as being under the influence of the Russians. Under such a condition, *Poland* was identified not with the state, but with the consciousness of the people, especially with language, religion, and national history. At times, actions taken by Solidarity were attempts to strengthen this collective consciousness, such as announcing the intention to publish booklets for the teaching of a revised version of Polish history (Touraine et al. 1983:140). At times, expressions of nationalism were anti-Semitic (Touraine et al. 1983:157).

Solidarity, then, was a multifaceted movement. In the language of this work, the movement sought both libertarian and socialist goals. In addition, Solidarity was a nationalist movement struggling for national autonomy and promoting national pride.

Solidarity and the Church

Solidarity always associated itself with symbols of Catholicism. In 1980 at Gdansk, "the agreement between Solidarity and the authorities was signed by Walesa using an outsize pen adorned with a portrait of the Pope" (Pomian-Srzednicki 1982:145; *see also* Kennedy and Simon 1983:129, 140). In part, Solidarity's use of religious symbolism expressed the personal religiosity of union members. In addition, Catholicism offered a set of symbols and rituals which expressed opposition to the current social situation, which the government did not believe itself strong enough to suppress, and which were therefore available to other protesting groups.

The social teaching of Catholicism significantly influenced Solidarity leaders. A draft program for the first Solidarity Congress appeared in April 1981 and acknowledged four primary sources of influence: "the nation's best traditions, Christianity's ethical principles, democracy's political mandate, and socialist social thought" (quoted in Mason 1984:123). The final 11-page program issued in October of the same year contained no reference to socialism but referred to "Christian ethics, our national working-class tradition, and the democratic tradition of the world of labor." The program noted that "John Paul II's encyclical on human labor (*Laborem Exercens*) is a fresh source of encouragement" (Solidarity 1982b:206).

Understandably, Solidarity did not attempt a critique of the religious institution similar to what was carried out of other institutions. In the 1981 program adopted by the first Solidarity National Congress, there is no analysis of the church (Solidarity 1982b). In 1985, underground Solidarity issued *Poland Five Years After August*, which was devoted primarily to economic issues, although there were also discussions of "Law and Legality" and "Education, Science, and Culture." The Table of Contents contained no reference to the religious institution (Uncensored Poland 1985c). An English summary of the report's final chapter included only these comments on religion:

> Solidarity has proved that Poles adopted certain values firmly, such as regard for truth, human dignity, family, and religion. The strengthening of the Catholic church is an important element in this evolution (Uncensored Poland 1985d:16).

> [The church] has become a depository of the Polish national culture. It has become an integrating force for the people. The moral authority of the Church and the Pope is of the highest order—paradoxically even for the authorities (Uncensored Poland 1985d:17–18).

All in all, Solidarity was soft on the church. Although some union members criticized the importance of self-interest in guiding church policy formation, generally Solidarity used Catholic symbolism and acted to strengthen the church's social position. Piwowarski found that clericalism was a big problem for the Polish church. Priests still perceived parishioners as a passive mass: "Our church is still dominated by the clerical model. It is manifested in the reign of priests and their leading role in the church" (1984:42). Solidarity gave no public attention to this problem. Solidarity needed the church.

The Church and Solidarity

Did the hierarchy support Solidarity's goals? The bishops clearly expressed approval of the workers' right to form free unions, criticized government attempts to weaken workers' councils (which gave workers some power at the workplace), and supported the right of workers to change jobs without prior approval of management (Solidarity 1984:5–18). A difficult question is whether the hierarchy supported the socialist goals of Solidarity. A Polish Jesuit, Father Josef Tischner, who served as a chaplain to Solidarity and who was considered an extremist priest by the government, understood there to be an antipathy between socialism and Christianity (Tischner 1984:49; *see also* Kostecki 1985:38; Solidarity 1984:51; Kaufman 1986b).

The hierarchy—and especially its leader, Cardinal Glemp—does not speak for all Polish Catholics. "Both in the Church and in Polish society there is a significantly widespread view of 'the good Pope' and 'the bad Primate'" (Kaufman 1987:Y8). According to a description published in the underground press of a meeting between Glemp and three hundred priests in 1982, the following points were raised.

> Young people have become apathetic said a priest and say that it is more important to be human than to be Christian whereas the Primate always stresses religion at the expense of humanity. The Primate denounced this attitude as political and likened it to the pernicious preachings of the 'theologians of liberation' in Latin America (Solidarity 1984:28–29).

There were Catholics who wanted the church to modernize itself and to form coalitions with others seeking a more humane society. The primate denounced such people as followers of Liberation Theology.

Regarding workers' tactics, the episcopate was a force for moderation, emphasizing the need for peace and internal stability. When the workers at Gdansk struck, the initial reaction of the episcopate was cautious, and at one point the Bishop of Gdansk called on the workers to end the strike. Eventually, the hierarchy gave its support to the strike but urged moderation (Touraine et al. 1983:39).

In 1982, Cardinal Glemp opposed a nationwide strike called as a protest against the de-registration of Solidarity, and he was partially blamed for the poor support for the strike (Solidarity 1984:26). In November 1984, after a meeting between Walesa and Primate Glemp, the church required the "depoliticization" of religious meetings. At a workers' mass attended by ten thousand people, "monks suggested that the crowd take down the scores of red and white Solidarity banners on display" (New Statesman 1984:24). Cardinal Glemp later said:

> The Church is supporting Solidarity not as an ally but as a defender of human rights.... We do not want to dominate Solidarity, but we are ready to defend it if human rights are violated.... The Church will counsel moderation and restraint in any conflict situation (quoted in Kennedy and Simon 1983:142).

In October 1984 a priest, Father Popieluszko, was picked up by secret police from the Department for Religious Affairs of the Ministry of the Interior, and several days later his "brutally battered body" was raised out of a reservoir (Popieluszko 1985:62). Several secret police personnel were arrested, tried, and given jail sentences for this crime. Father Popieluszko instantly became a martyr. His funeral was attended by a quarter of a million people. He is referred to as the 'popular patron' of Solidarity.

This priest wanted a more political church. In June 1984, elections were held for positions on the people's councils. The bishops remained neutral because the elections were a political event. Father Popieluszko, however, denounced those who were going to participate in the election, accusing them of doing so out of fear or to avoid "inconvenience." Such confrontations with the government were sharply criticized by the official Church (Monticone 1986:190; Uncensored Poland 1985a:21).

Beginning in 1984, the official church disassociated itself from the socialist movement. Primate Glemp said the church would no longer support Solidarity (Monticone 1986:186). During the same year, nine people went on a hunger strike to protest Glemp's transfer of a pro-Solidarity priest to a rural town. "It was the first hunger strike in Polish history to protest a decision of a primate" (Monticone 1986:185).

> In an interview...on March 13, 1984, Glemp said that the task of the Church is to unite those who are disunited. For this reason, the Church cannot commit itself to either the political opposition or to the authorities in Poland.... (Monticone 1986:186).

It was reported that continued talks between the government and the bishops about church issues had been accompanied by a lessened interest with political matters among the bishops (Kaufman 1986a). Primate Glemp warned priests not to concern themselves with politics (Monticone 1986:185).

The bishops, of course, had their own agenda—"a relaxation of restrictions for permits to construct churches, greater opportunities for pastoral work, the relaxation of censorship, and the observance of full human and civil rights by the state" (Kennedy and Simon 1983:136). During the eighties, church leaders carried out their own bargaining process with the government in the pursuit of church goals. In 1981, the church won concessions from the state. The mass was broadcast on television, nuns were once more used as nurses in state hospitals, church publications were allowed to increase, and church construction increased (Szymanski 1984:126). In 1986, a former Solidarity leader was quoted as follows:

> We know the hierarchy is eager to have the Pope visit Gdansk next summer [1987] and that the Government wants him to go elsewhere. We are concerned that there are forces in the Church who would pay any price for the papal visit (Kaufman 1986a:E2).

Pope John did visit Poland the following summer.

In 1988, there were numerous strikes over economic conditions. The bishops offered to mediate the strikes. Subsequently, the church and the government reached agreement on giving legal recognition to the Polish Catholic church and on establishing diplomatic relations between Poland and the Vatican. in May 1988, when the government finally put down the strikes by the use of force, the bishops did denounce this behavior (Newman 1988).

In mid-1986, Cardinal Glemp commented that "Solidarity had changed from a labor union to a political organization and that the Church had no interest in politics" (Kaufman 1986a:E2). This excuse for a lack of interest in Solidarity is unconvincing. The Polish church, in fact, was quite political. In December 1986, the Polish government announced the formation of a "consultative council," which was to advise the Council of State, a body which had "only limited powers in Poland's Communist system" (New York Times 1986d:Y9). Originally, the government wanted to have the new council composed of ten members chosen by the Communist party, ten nonpolitical members such as university professors, and ten members nominated by the church. However, Cardinal Glemp refused to actually nominate anyone. Instead, he encouraged lay Catholics to participate. Solidarity supporters declined to join the council. Supposedly, the Cardinal's behavior allowed the church to avoid playing a political role.

In retrospect, it is clear that the government pursued a variety of policies during the eighties meant to weaken, if not destroy, the Solidarity movement. One strategy was to gain the cooperation of the church, which was perceived as a moderating influence on Solidarity. A compatible view was held by some Solidarity members who questioned attempts by bishops to discourage militancy and suggested that the church gained the most from the workers' struggle (Touraine et al. 1983:47). During 1988, the state allowed the church to use foreign money to organize several economic projects. A politically independent economist commented at the time: "As long as it [a social program] goes under the protection of the Church, the state isn't afraid" (quoted in Newman 1988:18). In May 1989, the Communist government legalized the church, restored the properties previously nationalized by Communist regimes, and generally freed church media and organizations from government interference (Diehl 1989).

During this time, the church's actions were also influenced by its self-identification with the nation. While meditating between the government and Solidarity, "the Church was always concerned with the fate of the nation. It tried to represent community and transcendental values...." (Bingen 1984:221–222). In November 1980, Walesa and other leaders of Solidarity met with Cardinal Wyszinski, who "warned the unionists to maintain a proper hierarchy of values in their activities: the nation should be thought of as the first priority, then society, then the state, and finally the broad sphere of human labor" (Bingen 1984:223).

In sum, during the eighties, although the Catholic church supported workers, its commitment to Solidarity was at best highly qualified. Two factors were important in the creation of this situation. First, the church persisted in seeing itself as above politics, above conflict. It viewed itself as a voice for the entire nation and thus as a force for moderation. Second, as a social institution, the church's self-interest did not always coincide with Solidarity's self-interest; thus, the goals of these two groups were not always compatible. Government policy tried to exploit this fact and to use the church to weaken Solidarity. The state made concessions to the church, and this was accompanied by Primate Glemp's attempts to distance the church from Solidarity. As recently as the winter of 1987–1988, the Primate described Solidarity as a closed chapter of Poland's history (Tagliabue 1988a:41).

The Contemporary Polish Situation

By 1989, Poland was in an extraordinarily bad economic condition. Unrealistically low prices on basic goods were maintained by subsidies which drained the treasury. Except for Rumania, Poland's standard of living was the lowest in the Eastern Bloc (Tagliabue 1989a:E2). In 1988, striking workers had chanted: "There is no freedom without Solidarity" (Ash 1988:51). Finally, the state made Solidarity legal. Liberal changes in the Soviet Union, as well as continued economic pressure from the West, contributed to the reemergence of Solidarity (Schmemann 1989:Y3).

During the process leading to a change in government, the church continued to play a moderating role. When Walesa negotiated with the government, he requested assistance from the church. As a result, a bishop was assigned to accompany Walesa to the talks. He sat at the table with Walesa but said nothing and played no part in the discussions (Tagliabue 1988a:38). Reporting on the negotiation process, a reporter from *Izvestia* wrote that one reason for its occurrence was the church's encouragement of compromise (Clines 1989). In August, Cardinal Glemp met with General Jaruzelski and afterwards with the Soviet ambassador to Poland. The latter supposedly carried the message that "Moscow could live with a Solidarity-dominated government if the church could vouch for it," to which the Cardinal's answer was said to be "that it was willing to do so if the Prime Minister could be a stoutly loyal son of the Church, with strong ties to Solidarity...." (Tagliabue 1989d:24).

The Catholic church helped elect a Solidarity government. Church leaders tried to rally parishioners for Solidarity candidates (International Herald Tribune 1989). In addition, the hierarchy acted to defuse divisive political issues. In early 1989, an episcopal committee prepared a document that became the basis for a proposed law prohibiting abortion. In May, 70 or so deputies, many of whom described themselves as conservative supporters of Solidarity, spoke out in favor of the proposed statute on abortion. Church leaders initially gave their support to the new law. While parliament debated the proposal, there were protest marches against it and letter campaigns for it. Then Walesa and Cardinal Glemp met and issued a joint statement urging that abortion not be a campaign issue (Tagliabue 1989b). Subsequently, the proposed law was put aside (Brumberg 1989).

No doubt such accommodation will be only a temporary situation. The conservative side of Catholicism is becoming more visible. Toward the end of 1989, because of church pressure, several cinema clubs canceled showings of the film *The Last Temptation of Christ*. At about the same time, the screening of another film, this time in an ordinary movie theatre, was canceled because the movie was condemned by church authorities as pornographic. At present, political leaders avoid antagonizing the church. One commentator noted that, while it is praiseworthy to criticize Communist censorship, "You are a Stalinist reactionary if you don't like it when the Church does not allow you to watch a film (that's for starters) thereby violating your right to freedom of conscience and choice" (Zborski 1990:10).

Censorship brings the church into conflict with libertarian ideals. It is now being revealed that the incidents just mentioned represent nothing new. Recently, a journalist discussed what happened when the party, trying to please the church, allowed the expansion of

Catholic mass media during the eighties. Dissident journalists, who found employment with church periodicals and newspapers, learned that church and party treated them similarly. "We were expected to leave our conscience and our opinions at home and to deliver what the new employer wanted" (Pawlak 1990:17). Generally, social criticism was to be avoided, but especially if the criticism was directed at the church itself.

In 1984, Catholic nuns established a convent immediately outside the death camp at Auschwitz. This became the center of a controversy between Jews and Catholics as well as between Catholics who believed the action inappropriate and Catholics who defended it. Being among the latter group of Catholics, Cardinal Glemp complained:

> Do you, esteemed Jews, not see that your pronouncements against the nuns offend the feelings of all Poles, and our sovereignty, which has been achieved with such dignity? (quoted in Hausknecht 1990:101).

The Cardinal spoke "as a Pole" and on behalf of national sovereignty. A very critical article by a Polish Jew (Warszawski 1989) about the Cardinal's speech was not printed in Solidarity's weekly magazine because "we must be careful not to alienate our readers" (quoted in Brumberg 1990:34). However, Solidarity's daily newspaper had been critical of the Polish church's actions concerning the comment (Warszawski 1989:29). An American commentator, after assessing the Polish situation, concluded that anti-Semitism is alive in Poland and accused the church of doing very little at the level of popular culture to eliminate the problem (Brumberg 1990).

This association of nation and religion strengthens the place of the church in society but also has its dangers. In 1977, a Jesuit published an essay in a Polish periodical in which he attributed the greatness of Poland to its religion. "To separate Catholicism from Polishness, and religion and the Church from the state, is to destroy the very heart of the nation!" (quoted in Sroka 1983:220–221). This collapsing of ethnicity, nation, and religion into a single entity evoked from lay Catholics a pointed response which was printed in the same periodical. They wrote that to equate Catholicism and Poland meant depriving Poles "of a large part of our culture." In addition, they rejected chauvinism and emphasized the universality of Catholicism (Ostrowski and Lipski 1982:223–224).

At the start of the 1990s, the church is in a strong position. The party has lost power, and in the absence of this common oppression, the various groups that had united behind the Solidarity banner are moving apart (Staniszkis 1989). By comparison, the church seems strong and united. However, its popularity is endangered at this moment of apparent triumph. With the growth of a free-market strategy, libertarianism is likely to be increasingly stressed, and this will tend to turn the people against an authoritarian church willing to impose its morals on society. Such a conflict is made more likely by the continued commitment of the church to traditional morality, which more modern Poles are ceasing to accept. Finally, the nationalistic cloak worn by the church is disavowed by some, and (as shall be discussed at the end of the next chapter) it is likely to become a still greater problem in the future for the Polish Catholic church.

Conclusion

Consistent with my introductory analysis, modernization is associated with secularization in Poland. The concomitant popularity of the church occurred because Catholicism was part of the ethnic-nationalistic identity of the people, because in a totalitarian-like situation the church played many roles not reserved to it in a differentiated society, because of Communist party policy, and because the church accommodated socialist ideals. A recent analysis suggested that a future Social Democratic Polish party could build on Catholic social doctrine "which in the version proposed by John Paul II long ago verged upon the best of the Socialist idea" (Syski 1990).

The theoretical framework contains the proposition that state support for a religion increases its popularity, implying that state opposition would lessen religious popularity. But the Polish case requires a qualification of this proposition. On the one hand, the government did weaken the church through the use of its own socializing agencies, by the creation of alternative rituals, and by limiting church access to the people via the mass media. On the other hand, because the state was not perceived as representing the popular will, government suppression won sympathy for all churches.

The analysis of the Polish situation suggests that important factors limited the accommodation of the church to the Solidarity movement which embodied socialist aspirations. First, the church's self-image as representing the entire community—a legacy of medieval social thought—prevented the church from taking sides. The church's goal was to be above politics. Second, the clergy remained concerned about institutional well-being, which meant that the pursuance of church self-interest diluted any commitment to Solidarity's campaign.

In the nineties, it is possible that the church may lose popularity. Internal divisions will emerge. There are those who want the church to embrace liberal, humanistic values not specifically Catholic in nature. This is the attitude Primate Glemp likened to the preachings of Liberation theologians. The church's continued defense of traditional morality, such as its uncompromising stand on abortion, will revitalize "selective religiosity." Given that "perhaps the most distinguishing characteristic of the Solidarity social movement was its emphasis on self-management" (Mason 1989:54), it can be expected that this ideal will not die and that in time the idea of worker self-management may be applied to the religious institution. Finally, the nationalistic strain of Polish Catholicism, once a source of strength, may increasingly become a basis of division. These matters will be considered again after the Latin American case is discussed.

Catholicism and the Liberation Movement in Latin America

This chapter considers how the Catholic church responded to another social movement that supported socialist ideas, the Liberation Theology movement in Latin America. The Liberation movement began in Latin America, was given expression in the writings of Catholic theologians, and is rooted in the activities of so-called base Christian communities. The theology was publicly named by Gustavo Gutierrez, a Peruvian Jesuit, in his *A Theology of Liberation* (published in 1971, the English translation appeared two years later), which "became the single most widely discussed theological work of the decade" (Cox 1984:136).

To help understand why a socialist movement developed within Catholicism, this chapter begins with a discussion of the popularity of Latin Catholicism. Then the relationship between the church and the Liberation movement will be analyzed, including a comparison of how the church responded to Solidarity and the Liberationists. The chapter concludes with a discussion of the implications of the analyses of the Latin and Polish cases for the theoretical framework presented in the Introduction.

The Catholic Church in Latin America

In Latin America, Catholicism does not seem very popular. Only 10 to 20 percent of the population (varying by country) attend Catholic mass (Willems 1975:366). This is in part the result of a shortage of clergy (Cleary 1985:9), but inadequate staffing is only a partial explanation for low participation. Nominal Catholics come disproportionately from the lower class. Willems (1975:364) quoted Emile Pin's description of the situation in a Chilean town in the 1960s, suggesting it "would fit almost any urban environment in Latin America."

The priest is believed to be a member of a class other than that of the workers, for he does not live with them and does not maintain any contact with them. To them the Church is something totally alien. It is not a position of hostility, but of practically ignoring its existence. The Church is something for the rich and the women.

Unlike in Poland, other factors do not compensate for the alienation of the poor. Latin America comprises 24 different nations. Across and within these countries, there is a great deal of ethnic diversity (Reed, Suchlicki, and Harvey 1972). True of all these countries is their obvious connection with European culture and the dominance of Roman Catholicism, except in several small countries such as Barbados and Jamaica. But Latin American Catholicism is a religious overlay atop ethnically diverse populations, thus making it unlikely that there is any identity of Catholicism with ethnicity in Latin America.

Nor are the branches of Catholicism within the Latin countries symbols of nationalism. Most Latin nations achieved independence in the first half of the nineteenth century. At the time of these struggles, the Catholic church was closely linked with the European centers of power (Williams 1975:78). Thus, in the minds of the Latin people, the church is not positively associated with their struggles for independence.

In Latin America, Catholicism is not identified with ethnic groups or nation-states but with a social class. Since the period of independence began, Latin American politics has had two contending forces, conservatives and liberals, and the church has consistently sided with the former. The conservative faction served the interests of the landowners of consequence, who opposed democracy and favored European culture (Bannon, Miller, and Dunne 1977:312). Liberals, on the other hand, tended to favor the separation of church and state, public schools, divorce, and the confiscation of church property. When the conservatives ruled the state, political power was used to protect the social position of the church. The Latin church became dependent on government support—so much so, in fact, that analysts wrote about the "capture" of the church (Levine 1981:30–31).

In sum, because of the nature of the Latin population and of its political history, Catholicism has not gained popularity because of it being part of ethnic or national ideologies. Moreover, the church has been identified with the ruling class.

Meanwhile, the challenge of leftist movements over the last one hundred years led the Vatican to slowly revolutionize its social teaching. After 1930, the Catholic Action Movement, a worldwide Catholic phenomenon, took root in Latin America (Cleary 1985). This movement encouraged a more active role for the laity in the solution of world problems. It was aimed at key social groups that were being propagandized by Marxists and Protestant missionaries—peasants, workers, students, and intellectuals. As a bishop said, "Pope Pius XI did say that the Church had lost the industrial working class and must not also lose the rural class" (quoted in Adriance 1985:134). In the 1950s and 1960s, Catholic Actionists attempted to construct a "New Christendom" by promoting Christian newspapers, labor unions, political parties, and student organizations.

After Vatican II (1962 to 1965), the process of accommodating Latin Catholicism to the twentieth century accelerated (Levine 1981:34–35). At the convening of this council, Pope John expressed the hope that the council would make the church once again a "church of the poor" (Cox 1987:10). This orientation was accepted by the council, but it has been the Latin American church that has given meaning and force to the preferential option for the poor. In 1968, the Latin American Catholic bishops held their second General Conference in Medellin, Colombia. The bishops focused on the need for structural change to achieve social justice and committed themselves to awakening the masses so that they could become the masters of their fate. The bishops recognized the evil of sinful social structures that institutionalize injustice, oppression, and violence (Poblete 1980; Levine 1981).

Soon after this deepening of the commitment to the poor, Catholic leaders were pulled and pushed into an even more critical social role by the appearance of repressive governments. In countries such as Brazil, Bolivia, Chile, Argentina, and Peru, the church found itself to be the only institution inclined and able to defend human rights. Catholic organizations were formed in these countries to aid the victims of torture as well as the unemployed and to argue for such basic rights as the right to a fair trial (Smith 1980:183). During this period of repressive national governments, groups of bishops issued statements calling for the use of economic models that would produce a more equitable distribution of wealth and for the creation of intermediary institutions such as unions and political parties (Smith 1980:184). The oligarchical governments forced the church to take an oppositional role.

Moreover, church self-interest was threatened by political changes. In the name of preserving order, military governments expelled foreign priests and killed others who worked with the lower class. Symptomatic of the situation, in 1977, "leaflets appearing in rich San Salvador neighborhoods shrieked, 'Be a Patriot! Kill a Priest'" (Fogel 1985:177).

Bishops expressed a belief that the spread of politically conservative Protestant churches in Latin America was part of a political design conceived in the United States and supported in Latin America. It was suggested that right-wing governments favored such religious groups (in the granting of visas, for example) to thwart the progressive efforts of the church (Simons 1985). In 1986, the Brazilian bishops went even further and charged that spreading Protestant fundamentalism was part of the American government's strategy to tame Latin America (Woodward 1986:63). Thus, at least some of the hierarchy came to believe that the most serious threat to the church came from a combined force of religious and political conservatives. While Latin America has generally shifted away from political repression, the old pattern of political conservatives–Catholic church alliances has probably been permanently weakened.

Thus, by the late seventies, a basically unpopular church was faced in many Latin countries by a hostile state and a politically supported religious opposition. Not surprisingly, "According to recent studies, one-eighth of Latin America's 418 million people now belong to Protestant sects" (Woodward 1986:63). This is the social environment that has nurtured the Liberation Theology movement, which among other things is an attempt to gain the commitment of the nominal lower-class constituency of Latin American Catholicism.

The Liberation Movement

The Movement has two aspects: Liberation Theology and the Base Christian Communities. According to Liberation Theology, the will of God can be discerned in the course of history, and the theologian's task, therefore, is to find the meaning of history. In the third world, history reveals a struggle to achieve social justice in social environments that are fundamentally dehumanizing. Thus, Liberation theologians reject the existing situation and, siding with the oppressed, work to bring about a more just world (Gutierrez 1973). As a Liberationist pastor in a Filipino church said: "The 'Chosen People' is neither a race nor a nation; it is the poor, the oppressed, those for whom there is no more room in the society organized by men" (quoted in Hornsby-Smith 1985:18).

Bishop Oscar Romero, who was murdered on the altar steps of El Salvador's main cathedral, has become a symbol for the Liberation movement. Although not a theologian, his sermons communicated essential aspects of the movement's way of seeing the world. In Romero's opinion, to understand God's intention there are two aids—revelation and the insights of the poor. On the one hand, the Catholic church has a "transcendent ideology" that allows it to critique prevailing social ideologies such as Marxism and capitalism. On the other hand, insight into God's will can be gained by "putting ourselves alongside the poor and trying to bring life to them...." (Romero 1985:187).

This concern for the poor means neither a glorification of them nor a disinterest in other classes. It does mean, however, that all classes ought to orient their lives around the elimination of social injustice and the social liberation of the masses.

> To those who hold economic power, the Lord of the world says that they should not close their eyes selfishly to this situation. They should understand that only by sharing in justice and with those who do not have such power can they cooperate for the good of the country, and will they enjoy the peace and happiness that cannot come from wealth accumulated at the expense of others. *Listen to Him!* (Romero 1985:111).

In succeeding paragraphs, Romero made similar appeals to the middle class and to intellectuals, who should not become preoccupied with securing their income or "take refuge in an uncommitted knowledge...."

Liberation Theology not only takes sides; it also accepts the reality of class struggle (Gutierrez 1973:273). To reject the fact of class struggle is to side with the oppressors (275). Christians must think of unity as in the process of becoming and not as an accomplished event (138). The Liberation theologians emphasize that there is a struggle within the church as well as within society. Gutierrez (1973:118) quoted numerous statements from Catholic groups calling for changes in the church, including allowing priests to work in order to lessen their dependence on those with money. The Liberationists have called on the official church to change by divesting itself of supposedly unChristian traits. For example:

> Power confined to closed groups; vertical authority...secrecy; the denial of participation on the pretext of unity and discipline; the repression of critical thinking and liberation solidarity on the pretext of institutional security or for the sake of maintaining the established order (Munoz 1981:157).

The Liberationists exert pressure on the hierarchy to accept a more open, democratic model for the Catholic church.

Among the Liberationists, socialism is generally preferred to capitalism, but not in a doctrinaire manner. Socialism is perceived as a means of achieving freedom without selfishness (Gutierrez 1973:21, 32–36, 90). Gutierrez (1973:112) quoted with approval this statement issued by a priest group.

> We do not believe man will automatically become less self-ish, but we do maintain that where a socio-economic foundation for equality has been established, it is more possible to work realistically toward human solidarity than it is in a society torn asunder by inequity.

For the Liberationists, socialism generates less selfishness than does capitalism.

The Liberationists seek an international and national redistribution of power such that the masses gain greater control over their lives (Gutierrez 1973:88). Liberation theologians tend to accept the idea that the success of advanced societies depends on the continued exploitation of poor countries, which is done in a way that augments the wealth of the local elite. They conclude that there is a need to create a new world economic order structured to reduce international inequality (Levine 1981:45). This new order would include the nationalization of foreign-owned land and mineral wealth, the redistribution of land from the rich to the poor, "and a popularly based development of diversified products aimed at the needs of local consumers, rather than a global market of the elite...." (Ruether 1986:26). The basic idea is to liberate Latin American societies from the economic control of rich, Western countries.

Recent changes in Liberation Theology have made it more open and flexible. The theologians have become more aware of the importance of ethnic and gender factors.

Base Christian Communities

The shortage of clergy and the inability to depend on state help for church pastoral work turned the hierarchy to the use of experimental parish organizations (Cox 1984:113–114; Dussel 1981:79). Parish priests and other religious workers encouraged and organized a new type of neighborhood organizations that became known as "base communities." In the mid-1980s perhaps as many as two hundred thousand base communities shared these traits:

1. Although they may have been initiated by clergy, and priests or nuns may continue to share in the leadership, they have a signifi-

cant degree of lay control and direction, an ethos which is more egalitarian than the one found in most congregations and parishes.

2. There is an internal liturgical life of singing, prayer, and the sharing of bread and wine, sometimes informally but often in a eucharistic fashion. The base communities are places of festivity where the historic images of biblical faith are celebrated.

3. Study and critical analysis of the real life 'secular' situation in which the participants live in the light of the Bible's message becomes a basis for political engagement by the community and related groups as well as individuals (Cox 1984:108).

The base communities use the Bible and other church documents to understand the 'deep structure' of their situation and as a guide to deciding on actions to solve community problems.

Problems acted on by the base communities include water shortages, illegal housing, poor garbage collection, and natural disasters (Bruneau 1980:229; Cox 1984:130; Hewitt 1986). The groups have provided such services as paramedical training and literacy classes, and they have organized agrarian cooperatives. The average members of base communities are more conservative than the leaders. In a survey of base community members in Costa Rica, the vast majority accepted that their organizations should be concerned about economic issues, but the members were split on the desirability of church involvement in politics (Navarro 1984).

Within the movement, lay leaders are being cultivated. Along with learning skills (such as how to lead discussions and administer social groups), community members are experiencing participatory democracy (Cleary 1985:117). Base communities represent, in fact, a democratization of the Catholic church at the base. Cleary has claimed that the greatest achievement of the Latin American branch of Catholicism "is empowering lay persons to a degree and an extent unknown in most other regions of the world"(1985:126).

In sum, the crucial features of the Liberation Theology movement are: (1) priority is given to siding with the poor to restructure nation-states and the world into more just societies; (2) class conflict is accepted as an unavoidable feature of contemporary society and of Catholic church politics; (3) a socialist economy is believed more likely to be just; and (4) a commitment is made to democratize society and the church itself. As in the case of Solidarity, Liberation Theology embodies both libertarian and socialist values and goals. Unlike Solidarity, however, the Liberation theologians have strongly criticized church leaders for the authoritarian nature of the Catholic church.

The Church and Liberation Theology

More than in the case of Solidarity in Poland, it is necessary to discuss separately the reactions of the Vatican and those of Latin American bishops. Even when, in 1984, the Vatican issued a sharply critical attack on Liberation Theology, the Latin bishops were divided in their response (Simons 1984; Dionne 1984; Pasca 1986).

In September 1984, the Vatican released a statement concerning Liberation Theology that contained three major criticisms: (1) Liberation Theology is too dependent on Marxism; (2) the theologians wrongly assume that class struggle is necessary and that the church must take sides; and (3) Liberation Theology includes an intolerable attack on the legitimacy of the authoritarian structure of the Catholic church. The document also condemned the unjust conditions existing in Latin America, but by placing the blame on "owners bereft of social consciousness" and "the savage practices of some foreign capital interests," the writers implied that injustice was the result of sinful individuals not sinful structures (New York Times 1984a; Kamm 1984; Simons 1984).

Regarding the first point—the relationship between Liberation Theology and Marxism—little will be said. An American Catholic philosopher has criticized the simplistic analysis of Marxism in the statement: "The 'Marxism' that the document attributes to liberation theologians is one that only the Vatican believes exists" (Sheehan 1984:E23). Moreover, the veridicality of the Vatican's portrayal of Liberation Theology is questionable. For instance, Gutierrez has retorted that he does not advocate class struggle but the abolishment of the causes of such struggle (Goodman 1984). Another Liberationist commented that, although they do use Marxist ideas, "the result is no longer Marxism but simply a critical understanding of reality" (C. Boff 1986a:22). As Maduro (1987) put it, Marxism is one of the tool kits that Liberationists use in creating their own Christianity-based world view. However, this point is becoming less important because Marxist analysis has become less significant in Liberation works (Steinfels 1988).

The Issue of Class Struggle

In April 1986, the Vatican released the *Instruction on Christian Freedom and Liberation*, which was supposed to balance the earlier, negative commentary on Liberation Theology. The *Instruction* claimed that "those who are oppressed by poverty are the object of a love of preference on the part of the Church...." It was reported that this awkward phrasing replaced the previously used "preferential option for the poor" because the latter had come to imply that the church would politically support the social struggles of the poor (New York Times 1986a:Y11). Consistent with this interpretation, the *Instruction* noted that "the special option for the poor, far from being a sign of particularism, or sectarianism, manifests the universality of the church's being and mission. This option excludes no one" (New York Times 1986b:Y10). This option is not to be "a partisan choice and a *source of conflict*" (emphasis added).

Although the church is not to be a source of conflict, the *Instruction* recognized the need for structural change and political action. The basic problem is sin, which—although it is an act of a free person—can result in a structure that is a "social sin." Thus, it is "legitimate that those who suffer oppression on the part of the wealthy or the political powerful should take action, through morally licit means...."—which in extreme cases can include violence. But the document praised "passive resistance" as a means superior to violence and condemned a social struggle that seeks to eliminate the opposing class.

In a similar vein, the pope criticized clergy involvement in politics. The 1986 *Instruction* affirmed that it "is not for the pastors of the Church to intervene directly in the political construction and organization of social life." This job belongs to the laity "acting on their own initiative" (New York Times 1986b:Y10).

The official Catholic view of the church as above conflict is matched by a view of the state, when acting properly, as the representative of the common good. "The organizational church thinks of the state and deals with it on the basis of a medieval conception of the state as 'the administrator of the common good,' as looking out for the common welfare of its citizens" (Cleary 1985:165). Official Catholicism does not accept the Marxian view that the state is the tool of a ruling class or the more modern critique of state governments as vast bureaucracies primarily concerned with self-preservation. The military governments in power during the 1970s did turn many bishops against the existing state governments, but this seems to have been a temporary situation. Governments in the 1980s were less repressive, and the bishops were more conciliatory.

This official Catholic political philosophy was evident in the course of the Nicaraguan revolution. Before the overthrow of Somoza, the Nicaraguan bishops severely criticized the government, thus helping to pave the way for a new government. After the Sandinistas assumed power, the bishops issued another statement calling for political pluralism and urging the people to transcend political partisanship (Dodson 1986:94). That is to say, the normal situation is deemed to be one of competition for votes by parties, all of which accept the prevailing system. The bishops could not accept the need for a continuing revolution. Conflict, such as implied by the notion of class conflict, is at best a temporary response to an extreme situation in the official Catholic philosophy.

An analysis of the Mexican situation helps clarify Vatican thinking on political pastors. Mexican bishops distinguish two ways of 'doing politics': "One is by acting in public realms to promote the common good, and the other is by engaging in partisan activity favoring one political party" (Goulet 1988:4). Only the first kind of political activity is considered appropriate for the clergy. However, even in acting for the common good, only certain tactics are acceptable to the Vatican. In 1986, after an election viewed as illegitimate because of widespread corruption, Mexican bishops threatened to close the churches for one day in protest. However, the Vatican criticized such an act as provocative and likely to lead to more confrontation. The Mexican bishops, then, simply issued a statement condemning electoral fraud (Goulet 1988:7).

Latin bishops have not all acted in accordance with the stated policy. For example, on several occasions Archbishop Obando of Nicaragua gave support to the contras seeking to overthrow the Nicaraguan government. In 1985, he said a mass in Miami, Florida, that was attended by the Contra leadership, with whom the archbishop was willingly photographed (O'Brien 1986:50–51). In a 1986 *Washington Post* editorial, the Cardinal portrayed the Nicaraguan situation in language characteristic of the contras (e.g., the fighting is a "civil war") and suggested that the government lacked popular support (Obando y Bravo 1986). However, in late 1986, the Vatican pressured Cardinal Obando to cease giving sermons that were so provocative of the Nicaraguan government (Lernoux 1989:18).

Whether or not a government's actions are for the common good is decided by the hierarchy. In 1986, the Vatican condemned Nicaragua's expulsion of Bishop Pablo Antonio Vega as a violation of religious freedom. The government, however, said that the punishment was a reaction to the bishop's political activity.

> The Nicaraguan Embassy asserted that Bishop Vega celebrated a mass [in Honduras] attended by 200 anti-Government guerrillas...and encouraged them to act with "faith and resolu-

tion." According to the statement Bishop Vega told the guerril-
las: "You don't have to be afraid of the Sandinista Government"
(Dionne 1986:Y6).

The pope himself condemned the expulsion as recalling the "dark
ages" of Latin American anti-clericalism, but what the Pope described
as anti-clericalism, the Sandinistas understood to be an act of political
self-defense against an enemy of the state.

In the end, Rome judges whether or not government action is
legitimate, and if the judgement is negative, then it appears permissi-
ble for the hierarchy to be political. The Bishop Vega incident suggests
that acts directed against the church are not likely to be perceived as
for the common good. That is to say, church self-interest affects
whether or not political opposition to a government will be judged
fitting for the Catholic church.

In Latin America, then, the Vatican generally seems willing to
accept only that political activity by the clergy which is above class
interest. An example occurred in May 1989. After General Noriega
annulled a presidential election in which he was defeated, the Pana-
manian hierarchy condemned the regime and asked soldiers to dis-
obey illegal orders (Gruson 1989). David Levine wrote: "The bishops
fear that redefinition of the Church's base in class terms effectively
precludes appealing to all social groups and bringing all social classes
a message of salvation" (1986:250).

This Vatican position collides with the Liberationists' endorsement of siding with the poor. Understandably, the pope condemned
the participation of priests in the Nicaraguan cabinet (Dodson
1986:98). The Liberation movement favors a politically active partisanship that is unacceptable to Rome.

The Issue of Church Structure

In 1981 a Brazilian priest, Leonardo Boff, published *Church:
Charism and Power* in Portuguese, which was condemned by an arch-
diocesan tribunal of the Catholic church in Rio de Janeiro, and for
which he was reprimanded by the Vatican in 1985. Better than anything else, this work makes clear why the hierarchy, and especially
the Vatican, cannot accept Liberation Theology.

The Vatican's handling of Father Boff's case illustrates the lack
of due process within the church. Were it not for the pope's intervention, the Sacred Congregation for the Doctrine of the Faith would
have made public its criticism of Father Boff without any previous
consultation with him (Boff 1986:89). The Vatican was criticized by

some church leaders for this as well as for not having contacted the Brazilian Bishop's Conference prior to the public criticism of Father Boff. The President of the National Conference of Brazilian Bishops questioned the authoritarian manner in which the Boff affair had been carried out (C. Boff 1986:97). Clodovis Boff suggested that his brother's case has raised consciousness about the importance of "human rights for Christians too" (C. Boff 1986:99).

In his book, Father Boff presented a historical analysis of church organization which I shall briefly summarize here. At the end of the colonial period, the church allied itself with the ruling classes who controlled the state. However, it also desired to serve the mass of people who are poor. Thus, the church educated the children of the powerful to be compassionate, and it established various assistance programs for the poor. This Boff called a church *for* the poor. In recent years, this type of church "denounced the abuses of the capitalist system and the marginalization of the poor. However, it did not present an alternative perspective but a reformist one, acceptable to the dominant sectors of society" (Boff 1985:6). In the 1970s, a new model for the church appeared. Religious leaders opted for the poor: "They began to enter the world of the poor, embracing their culture, giving expression to their claims, and organizing activities that were considered subversive by the forces of the status quo" (8). The new model is a church *of* and *with* the poor. It seeks basic societal changes in the distribution of power.

With this change in role, the church is supposedly undergoing a change in structure. Father Boff portrayed as outdated such organizational traits as centralization of power, sexual discrimination, internal censorship, and the absence of democratic appeal procedures. He quoted the authoritarian view of a nineteenth-century pope: "No one can deny that the Church is an unequal society in which God destined some to be governors and others to be servants. The latter are the laity; the former, the clergy" (142). In such a church, holiness is equated with compliance. "As a result, almost all of the modern saints are saints of the system: priests, bishops, and religious; there are few lay people and even those few were captured by the central ruling power" (114). Boff suggested that the new church will be democratic, fraternal, and emphasize the participation of all members in decision-making.

Such was the message in Father Boff's book. Undoubtedly, the church continues to resist the democratization of itself. The lack of internal due process appeared not only in the handling of the Boff case. In 1981, the Nicaraguan bishops ordered priests in the national cabinet to resign without discussing the matter with the affected priests (Dodson 1986:98). "The real issue in Nicaragua is not Marxism versus religion, but democratization in church and polity" (Dodson 1986:48).

Insight into how the Vatican can both champion democracy and be authoritarian can be gained from the current pope's discussion in 1987 of the Chilean situation:

> Asked if he expected to help bring about democracy in Chile, the Pope said: "Yes, yes, I am not the evangelizer of democracy, I am the evangelizer of the Gospel." To the Gospel message, of course, belongs all the problems of human rights, and if democracy means human rights it also belongs to the message of the Church (Suro 1987a:Y7).

The pope distinguished between human rights and democracy. He identified the church primarily with the defense of human rights, secondarily with support for a democratic political system. If the pope believes, as I think he does, that the church is changing so as to preserve individual human rights, then the church need not become democratic. Such an analysis, however, cannot satisfy those influenced by the libertarian tradition.

A Comparison of the Polish and Latin Situations

Three points will be considered here: (1) the greater hostility of the Vatican toward Liberation Theology; (2) how government actions have influenced religious popularity; and (3) the relationship between religion and ethnicity.

The Church's Hostility Toward the Liberation Movement

The Vatican has reacted with hostility only toward the Liberation movement. Thus, there is a Vatican-led effort to rein in the popular base communities and to reinforce authoritarianism (Levine 1986:248–49; Dodson 1986:101). Concurrently, the Vatican has been appointing as new bishops men who are on the Vatican's side in the clash with Liberation Theology (Brooke 1989a). I suggest that the hierarchy's greater hostility toward the Liberation movement is a consequence of the direct critique of church structure by the Liberation theologians, of the use of a Marxist conflict model by the Liberationists, and of the hierarchy's greater fear of Communism than of Latin authoritarianism.

In Poland, Catholicism is more popular. Moreover, as a secular opposition movement in a repressive society, Solidarity needed the church. In contrast, the Liberation theologians sought to increase the appeal of Catholicism by changing the church. Understandably, given my framework, they wanted to accommodate the church to libertarian ideas. This has been condemned by a threatened hierarchy.

Moreover, the Liberationists argue that the poor have a privileged moral perspective. The American Protestant theologian Robert McAfee Brown drew the obvious conclusion from the assumption that the Bible is about the liberation of oppressed peoples: "It means that those who are in a similar situation of oppression today are likely to understand the heart of the Bible's radical message of justice better than those who approach the same texts from a position of privilege and have a vested interest in 'taming' the otherwise challenging biblical stories of upheaval and change" (Brown 1986:9). Within the religious institution itself, Liberation Theology diminishes the role of the hierarchy by elevating the religious role of the powerless.

In addition, Solidarity's conflict model, being liberal rather than Marxist, is more acceptable to church leaders. Both Solidarity and Liberation Theology use a conflict model of society. However, the nature of the model is not the same in the two cases. In Poland, social conflict involved Solidarity, the party, and the church. All supposedly represented the workers or were at least sympathetic to their cause. Given this fundamental similarity of interest, the Polish workers understandably sought political pluralism and structural differentiation—with the premise being that no group, including Solidarity, has a monopoly on truth. In Latin America, social conflict is perceived in terms of a local-international elite alliance versus the local poor. Marxist ideas are more useful in analyzing the Latin situation. The pluralist model, favored by Solidarity, allows a significant role for any religious hierarchy. The Marxist option diminishes the role of all current elites, including the religious elite.

Thus, hostility toward the Liberation movement is fueled by the opposition to diminishing the organizational power and moral pre-eminence of the church hierarchy.

Finally, the Vatican was more supportive of Solidarity because church leaders felt more threatened by Communist governments than by the repressive conservative governments of Latin America. In 1987, the pope visited both Chile under the dictator Pinochet and Communist Poland. The way he related to government leaders in the two countries was different:

In Chile, he saw General Pinochet in his palace, seeming to confer a kind of legitimacy on his presence in the seat of Government. Here [in Poland] he has seen General Jaruzelski only on neutral ground, although he has been much warmer and smiling in his treatment of his compatriot.

The key difference, however, is that in Chile the Pope embraced people who attacked the Government but did not do so himself, while in Poland he has explicitly criticized the regime, questioning its philosophical underpinnings and its treatment of workers. Moreover, he has forcefully praised the Solidarity Movement and has embraced as his own the ideals with which Solidarity challenged the Government.

In both Chile and Poland, he has called for patience and religious faith to bring about political change. But in Chile he pleaded with a vigorous and growing opposition movement to reject violence. In Poland, however, he urged people not to give up on the noble ideals they gave voice to a few years ago (Suro 1987b:Y8).

The explanation for these differences can be found in the pope's political analysis of Poland and Chile, given just before a visit to Chile.

Asked by a reporter today to compare the situations in Chile and in his native Poland, John Paul said, "We are going to encounter a system [in Chile] which is currently dictatorial but which is transitory by its own definition."

In Poland, he said, there are no signs that dictatorship will give way and so the struggle of the people there is "much more demanding and difficult" than in Chile (Suro 1987a:Y7).

This analysis appears naive. Even after Pinochet, one would expect concerted efforts by the Chilean elite and middle class to ensure that the government remains conservative in practice. The pope's analysis makes more sense if we think not of the working class but of the Catholic church. At the time, it seemed probable that antagonism toward bishops would last a shorter time in Chile than in Communist Poland. The pope's behavior in Chile and Poland makes sense in the light of church self-interest.

In sum, the greater hostility toward the Liberation movement occurred because, in various ways, the Liberation program would weaken the power of the hierarchy and because church leaders felt less threatened by Latin governments, even repressive ones, than by Communist regimes. The Liberationists strongly support the democratization of the church. Moreover, their theology gives a privileged, interpretative role to the powerless people, and their conflict model of society portrays the religious elite as (intentionally or not) on the side of the dominant economic class, which calls into question the validity of the hierarchy's pronouncements. All in all, the church's hostility toward the Liberation movement manifests efforts by a religious elite to have power. Whether such actions are justified by Catholic theology is a question beyond the scope of this book.

The State and Religious Popularity

In general, a hostile state is a threat to any church. Such a state can quite simply kill religious workers, as was a frequent occurrence in Latin America between 1975 and 1985. A hostile state can limit the resources available to a church, as when the Polish government limited church building permits, controlled the amount of paper going to Catholic periodicals, and so on. Perhaps the most important way states affect religion is in the struggle over control of the socialization process. In this struggle, even a neutral state is a threat to a religion. The state becomes even more of a threat when, as in Poland, the government mounts an anti-religion school and media campaign.

Thus, it is true that state opposition hurts religious organizations. However, as was seen in the Polish case, oppression by an unpopular government can create sympathy for a religious group. In other words, state hostility is less damaging to the extent a government is unpopular.

Moreover, repressive government may increase a religion's popularity by broadening the needs served by a church. In Poland and in Latin America, meaningful structural differentiation along with dissenting voluntary associations ceased to exist for a time. The Catholic church became an alternative society. The significance of this for the church becomes clear when the state of repression is lifted. In Latin America and in Poland, the appearance of secular, alternative organizations formed to seek social change is lessening the political usefulness of the church in both situations. Already in Latin America a decline of interest in base communities has occurred in part because of the presence of secular alternatives. For example, some base communities in Nicaragua have been absorbed by the government's political movement (Lernoux 1989:20). In Brazil, the return of democracy has meant that there are now secular alternatives to the base communities for social action. Political parties and labor unions lessen some of the need to protect and develop these communities (Hewitt 1989). Moreover, some religious leaders argue that scarce church resources no longer need to be spent in support of issues which now have secular advocates (Bruneau 1988:96). Thus, when a state co-opts nongovernmental groups, this opens up many opportunities for religious organizations to expand the services they provide, thereby increasing their popularity.

Religion, Ethnicity, and Nationalism

According to the theoretical framework, religious popularity increases when religion is part of ethnic and national identities. This proposition seems verified by the Polish case. However, developments in Latin America are calling into question the likelihood that Catholicism will be part of such group identities in the future.

The Liberationists defend the popular Catholicism of the Latin people, which includes public veneration of saints and religious processions. Father L. Boff (1986:86) did criticize certain aspects of popular Catholicism, specifically superstitious and magical practices. His view on popular religion reflects a conviction that all manifestations of Christianity are syncretic and that the present official forms are inadequate. "One comes to the conclusion that the future of Christianity depends on its ability to formulate new syncretisms. Its present cultural expression, from Greco-Roman-Germanic culture, belongs to a glorious past. The present seems to indicate that it will be definitively replaced by the new cultures that surround us" (L. Boff 1986:106). Father Boff is not praising a superficial mixture or juxtaposition of beliefs and rites from different religions. The syncretism he desires involves the use of local cultures to communicate a Christian message and the adoption/adaptation of elements of folk religions, all done in such a way as to maintain the Christian identity (L. Boff 1986:90–91).

The Liberationists' defense of popular religious practices is consistent with changes in Catholicism that began during the Second Vatican Council. During his visit to South America in 1987, the pope spoke briefly in Guarani, a native Indian language, during a speech in northern Argentina. In effect, he gave approval to local religious customs such as "a huge annual procession for a virgin known as the Queen of the Guaranis" (Indianapolis Star 1987). 'Popular religiosity' is even being promoted by conservative bishops as a means of combating Protestant evangelizing. A conservative Brazilian bishop, newly appointed by the Vatican, intends to promote popular religiosity by supporting pilgrimages, pageantry, and street processions on

saints' days (Brooke 1989b:Y4). Recently, a *New York Times* reporter
compared the missionary style of some American evangelical missionaries and that of the Catholic church in a remote area of Paraguay.
The evangelicals who staffed the New Tribes Mission sought quick
converts to Christianity and to "civilization." But, a local Catholic
bishop said his church's missionaries are required "to respect the
Indian culture and to evangelize within this culture.... This takes
much longer, above all because this means respecting their religious
belief" (quoted in Riding 1987:Y4).

Latin America is a culturally diverse environment. The church
has ceased attempting to impose a single, European culture. It now
accepts diversity and seeks to work through the varied cultures.
Indeed, given the international presence of Catholicism, it is understandable that this attitude finds favor in the Vatican. This approach
will allow the church to survive in a pluralistic world.

This global perspective means there is a countercurrent to the
historical linking of religion and culture that has occurred in some
societies such as in Poland. When the church says all local cultures are
equally useful as vehicles through which to express the heart of
Catholicism, it undermines the rationale for the passionate, as distinct
from a functional, identification of Catholicism with any one ethnic or
national group. This is happening in Poland (and elsewhere) where
the identification of ethnicity and religion has been criticized by some
Polish Catholics because it is too narrow a view of Polish culture and
because it reduces Catholicism to a local religion (Ostrowski and Lipski 1982).

In addition, political changes are calling into question the usefulness of nationalism. For instance, in an increasingly integrated
European community, nationalism can be a problem. In January 1990,
the Polish prime minister urged the creation of an all-European political structure—i.e., one embracing Western, Central, and Eastern
Europe. He viewed such a structure as a steppingstone to European
integration (Uncensored Poland 1990:12). Polish messianism is perhaps logically, but certainly not emotionally, compatible with such a
pan-European perspective.

In sum, one aspect of the modernization process is the emergence of a single, global society. At present, this is a direction, not a
fact. Still, those responsible for policy in multinational organizations
of any kind must develop a global strategy for success. For universal
religions, this has come to mean respecting diverse local cultures,
while at the same time co-opting them. When a religion is closely
identified with a single ethnic group, this can have short-term advan-

tages, as in Poland. However, what is happening in Latin America, and to a lesser extent in Poland, suggests that a religion in the modern world will be better off *not* being identified with a particular ethnic culture. Rather, worldwide success would seem more likely if a religion is ready to wear the local dress everywhere, while simultaneously emphasizing its universal essence.

This conclusion requires a modification of the theoretical model. It was stated previously that religious popularity increases to the extent a religion is part of an ethnic or national identity. Although this remains true, it must also be acknowledged that long-term success in a global environment pressures religions to sever identification with any one culture or nation.

General Limits to the Accommodation of the Church
to Socialist Movements

Although it is true that the Catholic church has been accommodating toward Solidarity, there are factors limiting the extent to which the Catholic church is likely to accommodate any socialist movement. These factors are church self-interest, the church's image of itself as above partisanship, and the church's failure to accommodate libertarian values.

What is meant by "church self-interest" is a concern about the sociopolitical situation of an official church. In both Poland and Latin America, the church has its own agenda which the leaders follow in negotiations with the state. Church leaders have used their mediating roles to enhance their own institution. This seems an inevitable consequence of structural differentiation.

The major difference, however, between the church and the two movements being considered concerns their images of society. Both Solidarity and Liberation Theology use a conflict model; the church does not. Catholic leaders tend to understand the church as being above any existing conflicts and therefore capable of knowing the common good. As a consequence, priests are expected to be sources of unification and to identify with no class, or all classes, which is the same thing. As the Latin bishops declared at their Puebla conference in 1979, priests are "ministers of unity" (Berryman 1980:76). In contrast, Father Gutierrez (1973:277) wrote: "To speak...of the priest as 'the man of unity' is to attempt to make him into a part of the prevailing system."

In 1985, Cardinal Obando discussed class differences during a sermon, and his remarks were later printed in a local paper:

> If you observe the sovereign law as it is presented in scrip-
> ture, "love your neighbor as yourself," you're doing very well.
> But if you make distinctions between persons, "you sin and the
> same law convicts you as transgressors" (James 2:8–9). Chris-
> tians should therefore not distinguish between the rich and the
> poor, the powerful and the humble. Any community that makes
> such distinctions cannot call itself Christian, because they are
> not based in the teachings of Christ, but inspired in the mentali-
> ty of this world; and unfortunately it is not difficult to become a
> victim of that poison (quoted in Reding 1987:Y6).

Although the church has not always acted in a manner consistent
with its self-image as being above politics, this self-image remains
important. It could be said that the church adopts this understanding
of its role out of self-interest. By saying that it represents the entire
community, the church can befriend all people and expect their support. This might well be a reason for the Catholic church's image of
itself. In addition, however, it cannot be ignored that, since its founding, Christianity has been identified with love. Throughout Western
history, *church* has been associated with the common good and the
community.
    A third factor concerns libertarianism. In Latin America, the fail-
ure of the church to become less authoritarian is quite clearly creating
conflict within the church. But internal democracy is not the only libertarian issue. Although the clergy is not united on this point, in both
Poland and Latin America, democratization of society has been
accompanied by the Catholic church assuming the role of public
defender of traditional values. The Polish situation has already been
described. In Latin America, the Brazilian clergy have renewed their
opposition to liberal laws concerning birth control, divorce, and abortion. The state banning of a controversial film on the life of the Virgin
Mary was rumored to be the result of church pressure (Bruneau
1988:92). Given that contemporary socialist movements are also libertarian movements, these attempts to use the state to enforce Vatican
morality is likely to antagonize movement members and strain relations between the church and socialist movements.

Conclusion

    The relative popularity of Polish and Latin American Catholi-
cism, as well as recent changes in the popularity of each branch of
Catholicism, are understandable in terms of my theoretical frame-

work. Secularism, desacralization, and structural differentiation have weakened the Catholic church. Moreover, state support or antagonism, the variety of needs served by a church, and the relationship of religion to ethnic and national identities have all affected the popularity of Catholicism. Finally, consistent with my analysis of religious commitment, church leaders believed they did not have the support of the lower classes, and to remedy this situation they accommodated Catholic social teaching to socialist values.

However, it must now be added that certain factors limit the extent of this accommodation. First, because powerful social groups will oppose such accommodation, the church will protect its self-interest and limit accommodation of socialism. Second, because the church has an image of itself as above politics, it will not accept under relatively normal conditions a conflict model of society, and this limits accommodation to socialism. Third, because contemporary socialist movements endorse not only socialist but also libertarian ideas, the church's authoritarian structure and willingness to use the state to enforce traditional morality alienates those in socialist movements. Currently, the Vatican seeks a monopoly over organizational power and prophetic influence.

The two case studies have also deepened our understanding of the theoretical propositions stated in the Introduction. Although it is true that state support is useful for a religious organization, government opposition can have some positive results. For one thing, the unavailability of state resources to churches may, as in Poland and Latin America, increase the motivation of religious leaders to win popular support. For another thing, opposition from an unpopular government may increase sympathy for a church and make the populace more receptive to religious messages. Moreover, when the state prevents the development of autonomous institutions, the opportunity is created for churches to satisfy a greater variety of needs which will add to their popularity.

Another tenet of the theoretical framework is that religious popularity is greater when religion is part of the ethnic or national identity. The Polish case study certainly provided support for this idea. However, developments in Latin America and Poland suggest that the growth of cosmopolitanism and global strategies will lessen the significance of this part of the theory in the future.

It is, of course, true that the Catholic church cannot be considered a typical liberal church. On the issue of the relationship between religion and socialist ideas, however, I do not believe this church differs greatly from mainline Protestantism or the liberal branches of other religions. However, within liberal Christianity, the Catholic church is deviant because of its refusal to accommodate church structure to libertarianism; this makes the accommodation to new socialist movements harder for Catholicism than for other parts of liberal Christianity.

There are limits, then, to how far a Christian religious organization, even a liberal one, will accommodate socialist movements. Of course, the significance of these factors for the popularity of a religion depends on the relative size of the working class in a population. In determining the size of this class, it must be remembered that I use the label *working class* to mean workers who feel unjustly deprived or relatively powerless. In any modern society, this is a significant number of people, but in more affluent, professionalized societies, this class will be less of a factor in determining religious popularity. That is to say, with affluence and professionalization, religious popularity is less a function of a church's accommodation to socialist ideas and more a function of the other factors in the theoretical model. In fact, as modernization advances, countercultural ideas gain clarity as well as coherence, and religious popularity becomes more dependent on the relation between a religion and the counterculture.

Part II

Christianity and the Counterculture

❖ ———————————————————————————————— ❖

❖ 3

What Is the Counterculture?

While in Eastern Europe and the third world the dominant challenge to Christianity comes from socialist movements, this is not true in Western Europe and the United States. In these more affluent societies, a counterculture is taking shape within the middle class, and religious alienation is predominantly a result of the perceived incompatibility between these relatively new ideas and established religion (Roof and Hadaway 1979:373). Such an analysis implies that the contemporary loss of religious popularity in the United States can be reversed only if religious groups can cope with the changes in cultural values that became visible during the 1960s (Roof 1978). However, Christians on the religious right contend that, by its very nature, the counterculture undermines Christianity. They argue that the proper response to the new values is to reaffirm Christian tradition, thereby regaining lost popularity.

The counterculture, then, has been met by accommodation and challenge. Chapter 4 concerns the accommodative response. The basic issue is whether there are limits to how much Christianity can accommodate the counterculture. Chapter 5 focuses on the fundamentalist challenge to the counterculture. The occurrence of such a challenge is not predicted by the theoretical framework. Thus, the basic topic will be how to explain the popular appeal of the fundamentalist reaffirmation of tradition. Then we will analyze whether there are limits to the appeal of fundamentalism. Before these tasks can be undertaken, however, the nature of the counterculture must be outlined.

There is no clear, shared agreement as to what constitutes American counterculture. Over the past one hundred years, socialist ideas have found expression in numerous organizations whose members have clarified and rationalized the content of the socialist ideational set. This has not yet happened for the countercultural ideational set. Part II, then, begins with a discussion of the nature of the contemporary countercultural revolution. Just as the discussion of socialist ideas focused on countries where such ideas were especially significant, so the discussion of the counterculture will focus on the United States.

What Is the Counterculture?

Around the world, but especially in the United States, the decade of the sixties is considered a watershed in the development of the counterculture. No one can dispute the importance of the sixties, but the extent to which the ideas associated with this decade were new is open for discussion. There are historical periods during which established organizations and establishment culture lose their grip on the populace and—as in a suddenly rain-drenched arid area—a myriad of unexpected intellectual plants come to life and reveal their previously dormant presence. The rain gives life to new shoots and old shrubs equally. Similarly, in human societies, the social ground may open up, and all kinds of ideas surface and become visible. A cultural revolution such as the one that took place in the sixties is not an organized campaign on behalf of an integrated ideology but more a period of cultural chaos.

The scholar has the task of finding some order within what seems chaotic. Those who analyze the sixties usually separate cultural developments into two branches—the hippies and the New Left. During the seventies, a related movement took form called the New Age movement. I consider the New Age movement to be a continuation and elaboration of countercultural ideas that had been popularized during the sixties. In what follows therefore, these three movements are considered to be manifestations of the same underlying counterculture. Four themes of the counterculture will be discussed: libertarianism, the alternative tradition, self-realization, and the affluence ethic.

Theme One: Libertarianism

A major part of what happened in the sixties involved the reappearance of radical libertarianism. To make this point, first, there follows a brief discussion of the English revolutionary period, for at that time radical libertarianism was discernible. Second, events from the past thirty years are discussed which can be interpreted as fresh expressions of this same libertarianism.

The libertarian ideational set was forcefully expressed during the period of the English revolution in the years 1640 to 1660. Although popular revolts had been occurring in England for several centuries, "the middle decades of the seventeenth century saw the greatest upheaval that has yet occurred in Britain" (Hill 1975:13). What happened then has continued to influence both British and, as shall become clear, American history. During the years 1640 to 1660, two revolutions were actually occurring. There was the Puritan revolt led by Cromwell, which was eventually successful. The Puritan goals included establishing the Protestant ethic, securing the right of private property against the state, and gaining political power for the emerging, propertied middle class. Opposed both to this culture and to the old aristocratic culture were the ideas of people called Levellers, Diggers, Ranters, Quakers, and Baptists, all of whom sought to permanently turn the world upside down. They challenged the political, economic, familial, and religious institutions: "There was a great overturning, questioning, revaluing, of everything...." (Hill 1975:190). The writings produced by members of these dissident groups significantly influenced the political leaders who founded the United States, and it is this 'revolt within the revolution' that is my subject.

Politically, the seventeenth-century revolutionaries sought greater popular sovereignty. The radicals wanted to lessen the dependence of common people on all specialists. Just as they wanted simple, understandable law codes to make lawyers and judges unnecessary, so they wanted medical and pharmacological texts translated into English so that people would be less dependent on physicians (Hill 1975:299; Manning 1986). In the revolutionaries' world, each person would be his or her own merchant, lawyer, parson, and doctor —each would be free.

The radicals sought to eliminate poverty and gross economic inequality. Putting this program into practice, the Diggers occupied commons and wastelands and began to dig (i.e., cultivate) them without permission of the authorities. They condemned private ownership, the payment of rent, and wage labor (Aylmer 1986:98–100).

The radical revolt also sought to change family life. The rebels wanted marriage to be only a civil ceremony and to be done not for monetary reasons but only for love. They wanted to allow divorce freely and favored broad sexual freedom. There was a refusal to show deference automatically "from the young to the old, from fathers to sons" (Hill 1975:189). In general, freedom and individual rights were understood to be relevant not only to politics and the economy but also to the family.

The belief in freedom and equality was the basis for a new religious program. Rebels interrupted sermons in order to criticize the ministers' remarks. In some new churches, group discussion was part of the service; after a sermon, a call for objections would be made. Religious enthusiasm—i.e., a belief that personal inspiration by the Holy Spirit supersedes all church or scriptural authority—was popular. Such doctrine was at the heart of early Quakerism, some members of which claimed the ability to heal and work miracles (Reay 1986:148). Diversity of sects meant diversity of biblical interpretations, ending for some a belief in the authority of the Bible itself. As a prominent revolutionary wrote: "It is the end of the authority of the Book; but by no means a return to the authority of tradition. It is simply the end of authority" (quoted in Hill 1975:267).

The 'revolt within the revolution' was an expression of the libertarian ideational set. The ideal was for each person to be dependent on no one else, but to the extent that this was not possible, social organizations were to be democratic and the state was to limit the accumulation of power by any one person. Even if one has only a vague sense of the contemporary counterculture, it must be clear that there is a great deal of similarity between the ideas just discussed and those promulgated in the sixties. The American counterculture has deep roots.

Libertarianism and the Counterculture

Hippies dropped out of the so-called straight world, supposedly a social space where work is meaningless as well as demeaning and life is controlled by the pursuit of money and things. They tried to create an alternative society in places such as the Haight-Ashbury section of San Francisco. For the hippies, dropping out of society was meant to be a positive act, a necessary precondition for establishing a new kind of society.

In part, hippie society was a restaging of English radicalism in modern costumes. In 1966, people in the Haight began hearing about "a group referring to themselves as Diggers after a seventeenth-century English sect of religious communists" (Perry 1985:82). In September of that year, there was trouble in the neighborhood. Police imposed a curfew. The Students for a Democratic Society, part of the New Left, called on Haight residents to violate the curfew. "The Diggers put up their own signs taking a third position, advising people to ignore the curfew and either walk around or stay indoors as they spontaneously wished" (Perry 1985:93). If anyone went to where the Diggers gave out free food or where they put on street theater and asked who was in charge, the response was "You are!" The Digger plot was to have people assume freedom, to have individuals ignore laws, customs, and institutions and to be free (Perry 1985:109). "The Diggers had the most thoroughly worked out, conscious ideology of any group in the Haight.... The Diggers were the epitome of the avant-garde" (Perry 1985:259).

Similarly, New Age people value independence as much as the seventeenth-century radicals. The acquisition of a broad range of work skills is sought as a means to increase self-reliance, thus reducing "the dependency upon specialists to handle the ordinary demands of everyday life...." (Elgin 1981:123). As one follower wrote: "I am more self-reliant.... Each step is progress in independence; freedom is the goal" (quoted in Elgin 1981:52). Thus, the movement is associated with an interest in entrepreneurial activity and the founding of small businesses (Elgin 1981:80).

The New Left was that part of the counterculture that was committed to libertarianism *and* accepted the continued existence of large social organizations. That is to say, these leftists valued freedom but assumed that individual self-sufficiency was unrealistic. What distinguished the New Left was the commitment to participatory democracy (Miller 1987:13). The spirit and meaning of participatory democracy has some connection with the English revolution. Whereas the Diggers were a model for some hippies, the Quakers served this role for leftists. Some leftists were exposed early in their lives to Quaker ideals through contact with conscientious objectors and civil rights workers who espoused Quaker ideas. Individuals influential in the development of Students for a Democratic Society (the New Left flagship) had Quaker backgrounds (e.g., Kenneth Boulding and Staughton Lynd). Thus, SDS-sponsored organizations tended to have what were considered Quaker features—i.e., rule-by-consensus, emphasis on moral suasion, and face-to-face discussion (Miller 1987:146, 206, 264).

What exactly was the nature of an organization in which participatory democracy was practiced? Miller has suggested there were two conflicting tendencies within the New Left. On the one hand, there were attempts to establish stable, democratic communities. Their traits included emphasis on discussion and dialogue leading to decisions based on a consensus, rotation of officers so no one person could amass power over time, and the use of referenda so that key decisions would need the approval of the general membership. On the other hand, for some leftists, participatory democracy meant valuing spontaneity, which translated into a rejection of having organization officers or a hierarchy of any kind (Miller 1987:146–148, 242–245).

Libertarianism, then, has been an important part of what is considered the counterculture. Hippies expressed a radical version of this ideational set that sought to ground freedom on self-sufficiency—if not of the individual then of the small group. The New Left, however, accepted the continued existence of large organizations. They fought for participatory democracy and emphasized that this process should be practiced not only in the public world, but also in our private lives.

However, in both hippie and leftist groups, a basic disagreement about the practical meaning of freedom has become clear. While some argued that freedom means being spontaneous, others equated freedom with democracy.[1]

Theme Two: The Alternative Tradition

Robert Ellwood, in trying to understand the variety of religious groups that coexist in the United States, has perceived a common source that has allowed him to group together many of these groups. He has suggested the existence of an alternative tradition in European history that is ultimately rooted in shamanistic religion and which has expressed itself in groups such as spiritualism, theosophy, Rosicrucianism, Gurdieff groups, Scientology, and witchcraft (Ellwood 1973). There is an obvious tie between the alternative tradition and the sixties in that the groups discussed by Ellwood gained new popularity during that period. There is, however, a deeper connection. Countercultural groups, in part, expressed beliefs and values from this alternative tradition. To make this point, first this tradition will be described, and then relevant aspects of the countercultural movement will be discussed.

Ellwood described European civilization as having two traditions, established religion (i.e., the Judeo-Christian religions) and alternative religion. The latter tends to be expressed in relatively temporary organizations led by charismatic figures. Thus, while specific alternative groups come and go, the tradition they express is a continuous part of European culture. The alternative tradition ascribes its importance to the superior wisdom available from its teachers, whose insights rest not on books or some authority but on personal experience. These experiences give the teachers in the alternative tradition charismatic authority.

In the alternative tradition, understanding is ultimately not the result of reasoning and cannot be adequately communicated in words. Theoretically, the experiential wisdom of the alternative tradition can be gained by anyone, especially if one participates in alternative rituals and uses ancient technical aids such as certain drugs (Ellwood 1973:14). Alternative rituals are occasions for stripping away commitment to the roles and rules of established society and for entering a 'dangerous' world without prescribed paths, but a world in which the participants experience new heights of communal being (Ellwood 1979:28–31). Unlike in the established religion, alternative rituals are occasions for gaining and displaying spiritual powers or gifts.

The greatest fruit of these practices is an altered state of consciousness. The ultimate achievement is insight into the true nature of reality. The manner in which Ellwood (1973:43) described the goal within the alternative tradition—expanding consciousness until a person "becomes mentally one with the whole cosmos"—expresses the connection within this tradition between wisdom and mysticism. To be enlightened is to know everything, to be everything.

Proportionately more of the teachers of the alternative tradition than of established religions are women (Ellwood 1979:32–41). Moreover, the tradition is culturally feminine in the sense that values considered feminine in Western culture, such as a shared sense of community, are important in the alternative tradition (Ellwood 1973:80).

The alternative tradition presents itself as the bearer of the deeper truth. It does not demand that its followers abandon the established tradition. Rather, followers need only accept that the alternative religion complements and completes the established ones.

In sum, the alternative tradition within European civilization has these aspects: charismatic authority, emphasis on gaining spiritual powers, a belief in a hidden wisdom that is potentially accessible to anyone (especially if one uses mind-altering techniques), a belief that the wise person experiences the oneness of all, and the self-perception that the alternative tradition complements and completes established religions. Moreover, the alternative tradition has women leaders and a feminine quality.

The Alternative Tradition and the Counterculture

When drug taking became relatively popular among young people during the sixties, it must be assumed that they were many reasons. Undoubtedly, some took drugs only because others were doing it, some because the authorities condemned it (and thus they could express a rebellious attitude), some because they were tired of life (if not of living) and were in search of oblivion, and some for adventurous reasons. No one knows all the reasons humans act in a certain way, and this is surely true regarding taking drugs. What I am interested in is not cataloging all the motives for using drugs, but rather understanding the sixties drug culture, the shared beliefs and values about drugs among the hippies.

Drugs were an important part of hippie life, and this was especially true of LSD. Consuming this drug was supposed to reveal new levels of reality, especially the level at which the union of all things was experienced. The tripper speaks of the "collapse of ego," by which he means:

a breakdown of the fears, anxieties, rationalizations, and phobias which have kept him from relating to others in a human way. He also speaks of sensing the life process in leaves, in flowers, in the earth, in himself. This process links all things, makes all things one (Howard 1969:49).

The drug LSD was talked about as if it were a love potion because of the closeness one feels with those who share the drug trip together (Wolfe 1968:283–284). As one hippie said: "I did feel that we had merged and become one in the true sense, that there was nothing that could separate us, and that it had meaning beyond anything that had ever been" (quoted in Wolfe 1968:275–276). As I have said, people use drugs for many reasons, but only some of these were valued and encouraged by hippie culture. It was believed that drugs could open one's mind to new experience, to new ways of sensing the world, and this was valued. In addition, some drugs were believed capable of revealing the underlying unity of all reality, and shared drug taking was considered a powerful means of developing interpersonal bonds. Such was the hippie drug culture.

There is an obvious affinity between the counterculture and the alternative tradition, and many counterculturists are aware of this. For example, they are interested in native Americans. There are more believers among New Age people than among the general population in telepathy, psychic healing, clairvoyance, and reincarnation (Ferguson 1980:420).

Counterculturists want to experience altered states of consciousness, which they associate with feelings of union, closeness, and love. To this end, an elaborate technology (much of which is quite old—certain drugs, mystical techniques, dancing, etc.) is employed. Its usage is meant to increase conscious participation in the way things really are. The experience of union is simultaneously the attainment of enlightenment.[2]

Theme Three: Self-Realization

Unlike the first two themes, this one is a relatively new part of American culture. However, it has roots as well. For over one hundred years, self-realization as a desirable goal for the members of a society has been part of the social science tradition (Bottomore 1964:243). What is new is the degree to which this goal has been socially recognized and linked to institutional developments.

After World War II, there took shape in the United States a

movement among mental health specialists that defined health in terms of self-realization. To be healthy meant to grow—to develop one's potentials—and this required self-exploration so that one would come to know who one was and who one was capable of becoming (Moustakis 1956). To be healthy in this way required a supportive social environment. If a person has open relationships with others, it is possible to share one's thoughts fearlessly, and this encourages being honest with oneself. In such relationships, a person receives the kind of feedback that deepens self-understanding. Thus, self-awareness, a prerequisite for realizing one's potential, is more likely in an environment where relationships are open and people are trusting.

Self-exploration and open communications were traits that distinguished hippie communes. Prototypical communes exemplified radical libertarianism and used the technology meant to achieve altered status of consciousness (Houriet 1972). In addition, the communes allowed and encouraged self-development. Much energy was used to plumb the depths of one's self and others. 'Schools' were to encourage individual creativity and self-development. Self-revelation and interpersonal understanding were important. As one commune member said: "We've learned how to be naked with one another...." (quoted in Houriet 1972:117). The psychologist Carl Rogers said that we may be living in the first society in which people are really open with each other (Ferguson 1980:35).

The pursuit of self-actualization is reaching new levels of sophistication in the New Age movement.

> [Followers] tend to work on developing the full spectrum of their potentials: physical (for example, running and yoga), emotional (learning the skills of intimacy and sharing with others), mental (developing both sides of the brain—both rational and intuitive faculties), and spiritual (allowing the totality of one's life experience to become a meditation) (Elgin 1981:36).

The range of influences and interests among New Age people is conveyed by this partial list of 'triggers' for personal development: biofeedback, improvisational theater, meditation, dream journals, theosophy, gestalt therapy, yoga, and mountain climbing (Ferguson 1980:86–87).

However, by itself this technology is insufficient. To grow, we require open relationships in which people aid and encourage and accept mutual growth. Although Robert Heinlein was in no way connected to the counterculture, his *Stranger in a Strange Land* (1961) became "the best-selling underground novel," according to its paper-back cover (Heinlein 1968). *Stranger in a Strange Land* added a new word to the American language. *Grok* is a slang word meaning "to under-stand thoroughly because of having empathy (with)" (*Webster's New World Dictionary of the American Language*, Second College Edition). Or, as a character in the novel explains, *grok* means "to understand so thor-oughly that the observer becomes a part of the observed—to merge, blend, intermarry, lose identity in group experience" (Heinlein 1968:206). *Groking* means perfect interpersonal understanding.

In the counterculture, then, people are to be free so that they can realize themselves. This self-realization depends on open relation-ships in which communication is the vital ingredient. The purposes of relationships are mutual personal growth and a degree of intimacy and identity symbolized by the term *groking*.

Theme Four: The Affluence Ethic

Another distinguishing aspect of the countercultural movement is an attitude toward material things. A self-styled former hippie dif-ferentiated so-called straight materialism from the hippie version. The straight materialist works to accumulate material goods but feels guilty about pleasure and is not committed to the art of living, to the elegant savoring of life's pleasures. The hippie materialist was described this way:

> We certainly enjoyed (nay, savored) gloriously electrified
> music, sumptuous repasts, cozy surroundings, exotic stimulants,
> well-designed tools, flashy costumes, nifty gadgets, and, above
> all, the voluptuous tits, asses, cunts, cocks, lips, hips, hair,
> ankles, and earlobes of our gorgeous lovers (Ward 1985:16).

The author advised: "Never deny yourself a pleasure in the name of a cause, an ideology, an abstraction" (Ward 1985:48).

Hippies rejected puritanical guilt about enjoying the non-saintly side of life. Physical things were appreciated not because they were status symbols, not only because they worked—but because they were beautiful or helped create beautiful experiences. The hippies returned us to our senses. But this did not mean the end of discriminatory judg-ments; rather, aesthetics served as a basis for making choices about how to live. Undoubtedly, and especially among youth seeking eman-cipation, pleasure tended to mean any sensual stimulation forbidden by those with authority. So orgies could be, and probably were, symbols of freedom. With time, however, what is pleasurable is no longer what is forbidden. The obvious truth that not all stimulation is pleasurable, then, forces individuals to make judgments about what is pleasurable. Hippies used aesthetic criteria for determining what the good life was. But this is still a revolutionary act. It expresses the aesthetic challenge to the historic dominance of brute force and moral norms. This is not to say that the counterculture replaced moral norms with aesthetic criteria. I claim only that this culture gave new legitimacy to using aesthetic principles as guides for living.

Among the New Age descendants of the hippies, it is popular to espouse the simple life, but that is not equated with the absence of things and pleasures. In the New Age movement, "Voluntary simplicity is an aesthetic simplicity...." (Elgin 1981:32). As one follower said: "I wanted a simplicity that would include beauty and creativity—art, music, literature, and aesthetic environment—but simply" (quoted in Elgin 1981:53).

Hippie culture contains an affluence ethic—i.e., a set of beliefs and values that are guides to leading an elegant life. While it is true that this ethic was not new in the sixties, it is true that the postwar economic success of the United States made the affluence ethic relevant for the first time to a majority of Americans. I suggest that the key to the affluence ethic is the elevation of aesthetic norms to be on a par with moral criteria.

In Sum: The Counterculture

By the term *counterculture*, then, I mean the resurfacing of the alternative tradition, the renewed, vigorous assertion of libertarian aspirations, the concern about self-realization, and the appearance of an affluence ethic.[3]

In their reinvention of the English revolution, the American counterculturists experienced the paradoxical nature of freedom. When you try to put it into practice, you understand that freedom has several ways of being expressed—the lone self-sufficient individual, the spontaneous happening, and the democratic group—and that such expressions are more or less mutually exclusive. The diverse meanings of freedom imply the existence of inconsistent ideals within the libertarian ideational set. I shall return to this subject later.

Because of its continued importance in modern societies, the alternative tradition must be added to the theoretical scheme presented at the end of the Introduction. All else being equal, given the continued appeal of the alternative tradition, if religions want to be popular, they would accommodate this tradition. The alternative tradition emphasizes a blend of magic and mysticism, the wisdom of shamanistic figures, and the underlying unity of all things. In this tradition, all established religions are considered of relatively equal value, needing to be completed by being founded on the experiential wisdom of the alternative tradition.

The succeeding two chapters focus on the responses within Christianity to the counterculture.

Christian Accommodation of the Counterculture

As discussed in the Introduction, the overall decline in church attendance and the increase in religious nonaffiliation that has occurred in the United States over the past thirty years has been linked to the appearance of the counterculture. However, analysts have usually been vague about the nature of this culture, often equating it with specific issue positions such as sexual freedom or the acceptance of legalized abortion. In the preceding chapter, I tried to specify the diverse strands of the new (and not-so-new) culture. Based on that analysis, it is suggested that the recent decline in religious popularity in the United States has resulted from the inadequate accommodation of religious institutions to a growing interest in the alternative tradition, radical libertarianism, personal growth, and an ethic that focuses on enjoying affluence.

However, it is also true that religious leaders have intuitively grasped the problem and made efforts to accommodate aspects of the counterculture. Because the manner in which Christianity responded to the counterculture is not only less widely known than the changes in Catholic social thought generated by the socialist challenge, but also because the religious responses to the counterculture are less well-understood to be such, it is necessary to describe the nature of these responses before considering what might limit the accommodation of Christianity to the counterculture.

The Alternative Tradition and Christianity

For the most part, I will be discussing recent changes within mainline Protestantism. However, one of the earliest responses to the appearance of the counterculture developed primarily within fundamentalist Protestantism, although it also became an important part of mainline Protestantism. I refer to the Jesus movement.

The Jesus Movement

Some people who became disillusioned with the sixties but who also could not return to mainstream culture joined the Jesus movement. This movement became a haven for the alienated. Starting in the late sixties, there were Christian coffeehouses, Jesus posters, Christian rock, and Christian communes. It was old-fashioned Pentecostal Christianity that tended to find favor among former hippies. Ellwood listed important similarities between the hippie and Pentecostal worlds—emphasis on personal experience of the really real (getting high on drugs, getting 'high' on Jesus), being outside the mainstream, belief in miracles and fascination with mysteries, and an identification of political struggle with a moral crusade (Ellwood 1973:18–20). In my terms, the Jesus movement shared attributes with the alternative tradition.

The Living Word Fellowship (LWF) is an example of the communes that were part of the Jesus movement. Most of the approximately three hundred members were young, lower middle-class whites. The commune was authoritarian in its structure and fundamentalist in its theology and morality. The world was perceived as a battleground for God and Satan. Those who sought peace or social unity were defined as unrealistic, if not evil.

While clearly a fundamentalist group, the Fellowship shared traits with the alternative tradition, as suggested by a member's comment:

> I used to think Indian tribes were real neat, and I wanted to be part of an Indian tribe. Communities like that, I wanted that. And here it was, just handed to me (quoted in Tipton 1982:68).

Tipton wrote: "This is certainly the first generation of sectarian Christians for whom their church is like 'an Indian tribe.'"

The Fellowship's founder and pastor was a woman. The unity of the Fellowship resulted from the members' subservience to the rules established by her. Tipton suggested several sources for the legitimation of the pastor's authority:

> First, her history shows signs of divine selection: prophetic 'anointment,' an ecstatic journey to the edge of death, and a miraculous recovery.... Second, she exercises extraordinary shamanistic powers of trance induction, healing, and psycholog-

ical insight, along with prophetic powers of interpretation and judgment.... (1982:62–63).

The manner of their selection and their spiritual powers are what has always legitimated shamans (Gill 1981). In addition, Tipton mentioned as sources of legitimacy the apparent consistency between the pastor's rules and biblical texts, her own adherence to sect rules, and her commitment to the members. What I want to emphasize, however, is the similarity between the pastor and the shaman.

The language of ecstasy was part of the Fellowship's culture. Through experiences such as speaking in tongues, ritual participants achieved a form of identity with the sacred in an emotional atmosphere that also evoked feelings of closeness with the other participants.

The Living Word Fellowship reflected both fundamentalism and the alternative tradition. The influence of the latter can be seen in the shamanlike role of the pastor, the valuing of direct contact with the sacred, and the prominence of spiritual gifts such as healing. However, the essentially Christian nature of the group was preserved by the pastor's dependence on the Bible. In sum, the Jesus movement was the Christianization of one part of the counterculture, the alternative tradition. The influence of the alternative tradition gained wider social significance with the rise to prominence of the charismatic movement, which is the Jesus movement in 'respectable' clothes.

The Charismatic Movement

The charismatic movement (or, as it is also called, the neo-Pentecostal movement) became a prominent part of American Christianity beginning in the sixties. It remains predominantly a middle-class movement that attracts followers from the classical Pentecostal churches such as the Assemblies of God, mainline Protestant churches, and Roman Catholicism (Flowers 1984). However, the movement is more Protestant than Catholic, more fundamentalist than liberal.

Unlike the earlier Pentecostal movement that began around the turn of the century, members of the charismatic movement are not all fundamentalists and their rituals are more emotionally restrained. The central ritual is a fellowship or prayer meeting, which is often held outside the regular service schedule of any church. These meetings involve prayer, Bible study, singing, and the giving of personal testimonies.

The prayer meeting is quite different from the average middle-class Sunday service. It is relatively spontaneous and free-flowing, and participants are encouraged to speak out, to express themselves physically, and to be enthusiastic—i.e., controlled displays of emotion such as clapping hands or raising arms are approved (Harder 1985:102). During these rituals, individuals display their possession of special gifts—notably speaking in tongues, healing, and even prophesy. Quebedeaux has pointed out that such demonstrations of religious power "were common occurrences in the shamanistic traditions of Africa, Latin America, and elsewhere long before the birth of the Pentecostal Movement" (1983:234).

In traditional societies, fasting was, among other things, a preparation for receiving sacred power. In a study of why contemporary people fast, it was found that charismatic Christians, more than others, reported that they fasted in order to gain spiritual power (Tamney 1986a). Charismatics interpret gifts such as healing as indicators of the presence of the Holy Spirit within them (Poloma 1983:4,51,60). Not unlike premodern people, for whom the alternative tradition was the established tradition, charismatics fast to gain the power of the Holy Spirit.

Those who excel in gaining such power are the "charismatic leaders" in the movement. Such a person

> 1) is recognized by others as possessing one or more of the spiritual gifts in special degree; 2) has a forceful personality, in that he or she, through preaching, prayer, and spiritual discernment, can evoke group experiences of Pentecostal power (including speaking in tongues, healing, and prophesy); and 3) is able, through personal qualities, to exercise leadership (Quebedeaux 1983:88).

There is an obvious resemblance between charismatic leaders and shamans.

Quebedeaux (1983:218) has acknowledged the tie between the counterculture and the charismatic movement. This movement can be seen as an attempt to accommodate the alternative tradition to middle-class Christianity. In both the alternative tradition and charismatic christianity: personal religious contact with the divine is the goal; the attainment of this experience means an increase in magical power such as being able to heal; these experiences occur within communal, enthusiastic rituals; and the leader is similar to the shaman.

In accommodating the alternative tradition, however, the charismatic movement changed its nature. First, among charismatics, spiritual powers are integrated into a Christian context. Actual prophesies rarely, if ever, contain new doctrinal revelations; rather, prophesies concern accounts of the working of the Spirit in the world—e.g., notice that a healing will occur. Moreover, charismatics have rarely "written down prophesies for fear that they could become permanent additions to the biblical cannon" (Quebedeaux 1983:134).

Second, the charismatic movement combines the alternative tradition and libertarianism. Individual clergy have played prominent roles in spreading and sustaining the movement, but lay people are more responsible than clergy for this religious phenomenon. The charismatic movement

> could be called the 'lay lib movement,' as it has witnessed the release of lay people into a great variety of ministries in the church which were previously regarded as the preserve of ordained ministers—leadership, healing and exorcism, preaching and teaching, and evangelism and traveling ministries (Harder 1985:105).

It is also true, however, that the lack of structure in the movement and in the prayer rituals has allowed individuals with strong personalities to become dominant in specific charismatic groups (Harder 1985:106). Even though the rituals are relatively spontaneous, over time the ritual of a specific group takes on a certain pattern and the group itself becomes structured, with certain individuals exercising leadership. In one charismatic group, it was a Catholic priest who had the important task toward the end of the ritual to discern the message contained in the evening's religious texts and individual prophesies, and who would give some concluding meaning to the ritual (Lane 1976:169). Occupying such an important position, someone could use it to gain control of a group.

Freedom is jeopardized by the absence of democratic structure. The accumulated political wisdom of Western civilization avers that freedom is best guaranteed by democratic rules. Yet, changes in religious ritual have favored spontaneity over democracy. Lay participation has increased in Christian rituals, but there is no necessary one-to-one relation between participation and power. Freedom requires the sharing of power, not simply of role performances. Freedom is related more to who determines ritual readings than to who reads them. Freedom is related more to shaping the shared understanding of a ritual event than to how much time a person 'has the floor.' In this way, there is a link between spontaneity and authoritarianism.

There is a latent inconsistency, therefore, within the charismatic movement between the importance of charismatic authority and the desire for lay liberation. In spite of this, it is true that the charismatic movement, more than the alternative tradition, shows the influence of libertarianism.

The Liberal Response to the Alternative Tradition: Mysticism

In recent history, there have been prominent, liberal Christians who have tried to integrate mystical ideas and practices into Christianity. Such people (e.g., Thomas Merton) were not part of the charismatic movement, although their interest in mysticism links them, like the charismatics, to the alternative tradition. Many years ago, Ernest Troeltsch (1931) made a relevant distinction between traditional mysticism and modern mysticism. A critical feature of the latter was that mystical practices were differentiated from magical practices. Although some Christians have tried to incorporate undifferentiated mysticism (i.e., the alternative tradition) into their form of Christianity, others have engaged in a similar process regarding differentiated mysticism. An example of the former is the charismatic movement; the latter response is exemplified by some mystics who have remained affiliated with liberal Christian churches.

Mysticism has appealed to liberals because it offers the experience of union. A prominent example of someone valuing mysticism precisely because it involves a sense of communal identity is William James. James wanted to define a religious position for a modern person, and mysticism had a place in his scheme. The ideal is to live in the 'strenuous mood'—a combination of ethical vigor and mystical experience. The primary purpose of life, according to James, is to enact an ethical code. James did not preach a specific ethic, but he assumed that trying to live in accordance with any set of ethical principles would be difficult (Browning 1980:213–215). Thus, James also valued mysticism, "when the knotty boundaries of the self dissolve and one senses a melting into a large unity with the world" (Browning 1980:252). James gave several reasons for the usefulness of mysticism: (1) ethics requires discipline which creates strain and tension, while mysticism means relaxation and indifference to the present which releases pent-up emotions; (2) mysticism gives security and support in the confusing world of modernity; feeling one with the world makes us realize there is an underlying unity in the obvious diversity; and (3) mysticism supports ethics by giving a natural ground for our sense of duty. That is, if we are mystics:

That person whom we help is not just a separate and foreign object we feel obligated toward; rather, he or she is someone to whom we feel related and attached. Our involvement with another person flows from our participation in the other's life and not simply from some arid sense of duty. For this reason, the mystical experience can charge the ethical act with a heightened sense of spontaneity and joy (Browning 1980:239).

For William James, therefore, mysticism appealed because it experientially affirms our relatedness to others, which allows us to feel relaxed and supported, and elicits from us spontaneously what ethical codes demand of us. James's appreciation of the benefits derived from the feeling of union with the world and of rooting ethical acts in this sense of relatedness link his philosophy to the alternative tradition. At the same time, James's philosophy is quite different from this tradition in that he espoused a differentiated mysticism and a mysticism subordinated to allegiance to a moral code.

There are other examples of significant twentieth-century Westerners who have praised mysticism. Teillard de Chardin (1961:285,295) valued mysticism because it connoted love and unity. In an interview with Eugene Kennedy, Joseph Campbell, the noted mythologist, referred to the "mystical theme of the space age." To paraphrase Campbell, the old age in which the earth was the center of the universe, in which love was reserved for members of the in-group, is passing away to be replaced by an age which realizes "the ubiquity of the divine presence in our neighbors, in our enemies, in all of us" (Kennedy 1979:52).

The appeal of mysticism to religious liberals is that, in a world of alienation and aloneness, it promises experiences of community and wholeness. Differentiated mysticism is a pale reflection, but still a reflection, of the alternative tradition. Modern mysticism appeals to people who cannot accept dependence on shaman-like leaders and do not aspire to magical powers, yet who yearn for a world that is healed and whole. In the space age, mysticism symbolizes the yearning for world wholeness. Among religious liberals, however, an appreciation of the experiential consequences of mystical experiences has a lesser place than commitment to an ethical code.

In sum, in direct and indirect ways, Christianity has responded to the appeal of the alternative tradition. The Jesus and charismatic movements co-opted many basic features of this tradition. Christian mystics have favored a part of the alternative tradition, namely the emphasis on the direct experience of wholeness. However, there are limits to how far even sympathetic Christians will adapt to the alternative tradition. The open-endedness of shamanism, in which new revelations are continually possible, is minimized once the alternative tradition is Christianized. In Christian groups, the authority of the Book is preserved. Moreover, within the alternative and Christian traditions different relative weights are given to spiritual powers and ethics. The absolute preeminence of an ethical code distinguishes the Christian tradition. Finally, as Christianity accommodates to libertarian ideals, it separates itself from the alternative tradition which remains committed to charismatic leadership.

Libertarianism and Liberal Christianity

The churches did not, indeed of their nature cannot, accommodate the radical libertarianism advocated by the Diggers and other hippie groups and communes. They did, however, show signs of trying to accommodate the New Left call for participatory democracy. This can be seen in some of the ritual changes that originated during the 1960s.

Ritual Renewal

Michael Ducey (1977) studied several churches in Chicago during the late sixties with an eye to describing and understanding changes going on in these religious groups. Ducey assumed that Western civilization is moving toward ever greater valuing and institutionalization of freedom, and so he examined the churches in relationship to freedom. Ducey focused on church rituals as occasions that graphically reveal the nature of religious organizations. He reported finding that a new type of ritual was developing, which he called "the interaction ritual." This ritual gave greater freedom to the lay participants than other existing Christian rituals.

In interaction ritual, the value given freedom is evidenced in several ways. First, during the ritual each individual is expected to tell about the personal meaning of the symbols presented; the purpose of the ritual is to discover new shared meanings through the free exchange of whatever reactions people have to the content of the ritual. Several times Ducey (1977:105,173) implied that free exchange meant spontaneous behavior by the participants, yet he also described the interaction ritual as rational rather than enthusiastic (Ducey 1977:163). Second, equality is reflected in the assignment of responsibilities; the "role of initiating sacred utterance or action is assigned by the congregation to various of its members at random" (Ducey 1977:7). Third, Ducey assumed that interaction rituals would occur in congregations in which the nature of future rituals would be discussed at formal meetings during which decisions would be democratically made (Ducey 1977:121). In Ducey's work, therefore, freedom has several meanings: spontaneous behavior during the ritual, rational discussion during the ritual and rotation of ritual roles, and a democratic planning process for the nature of the ritual. Ducey's interaction ritual means spontaneity, rough equality, democratic decision making, and interpersonal sharing leading to personal growth. Such a ritual would befit an organization fashioned in the countercultural mode.

Ducey discussed with church members the ritual performed at the Church of the Three Crosses, his model for the interaction type. Their comments conveyed the idea that the development of the interaction ritual was motivated by more than a desire for freedom. The ministers at Three Crosses changed from traditional ritual forms because they wanted a more involved laity; they sought to create a community (Ducey 1977:188). When discussing the appeal of interaction ritual, lay people mentioned the sense of freedom, but they also talked about the feeling of "real sharing" (139–140). The important point is that, although interaction ritual allowed a great deal of freedom, what stimulated the creation of the new ritual was primarily a desire for community.

Other churches in the sixties moved toward participatory democracy. "Grace Church" was the name given by a researcher to a San Francisco church. At Grace , the lay council had considerable authority, and much power was decentralized to committees. Sermons were sometimes replaced by group discussions (Wolfe 1976:238–239).

But, as in the case of the Church of the Three Crosses, the real meaning of changes at Grace Church did not relate to freedom. Grace Church created new rituals that were meant to have a nontraditional effect—fun. For example:

> The high point now of the church year is the annual Yule Feast, an extravagant celebration of the twelfth night of Christmas spiced with the wearing of Renaissance clothes, the burning of a yule log, the display and eating of a boar's head spiked with the drinking of wassail before, and wine during, a sumptuous meal (Wolfe 1976:232).

In the late sixties, Harvey Cox lamented the secularization of celebration and festivity. In the United States, festivals and celebrations had no religious meaning and occurred in secular settings such as football games and big parades. Cox used the term *festivity* to mean a social occasion characterized by:

1. The socially approved expression of normally neglected or sup-
    pressed feeling, or the accepted expression of what normally is
    considered excessive feeling

2. A sense of specialness—people dressing differently or eating
    unusual foods or unusual amounts of food; thus, the event is
    experienced as unconventional, different from the everyday

3. Concern only for the present—the festival has no purpose outside
    itself

4. Joyousness—the festival affirms life and gaiety (Cox 1969:22–24).

At its annual feast, Grace Church was reintegrating religion and festivity.

Similarly, Glide Church in San Francisco changed its Sunday
morning rituals from "services" to "celebrations." The church's
brochure explained what the change meant.

> We celebrate life here. We get close to each other here....
>
> Glide's Celebrations are all about involvement. It's difficult
> to be an observer in the Celebration's intense, joyful, intimate
> atmosphere. Two thousand swaying, stomping, and singing
> bodies color it. Flashing images and patterns expand it. Pulsing
> songs and sizzling music heighten it.

I attended a 9 A.M. "celebration" at Glide Church in 1987—some
20 years after the cultural revolution of the 1960s. The old Methodist
church had been stripped of conventional Christian symbolism,
except that the traditional stained glass windows remained. Banners
hanging from the ceiling were pretty to look at yet serious in their
verbal messages: peace, power, love, liberation, justice, dignity. The
celebration began with jazz musicians on the stage. At the same time,
slides were projected on the wall above them. The opening slide read:
"Nothing is more precious than freedom and independence."

But the celebration was more festive than revolutionary. The
hundred or so people of different races got into the music, which was
moving indeed. Traditional religious music was sung as well as secular songs. Some lyrics had been rewritten to stress the importance of
continuing the struggle for freedom and human rights. After the sermon, everyone sang "We Shall Overcome," joining hands and swaying
together. Like many sixties events, the Glide celebration helped participants to feel both righteous and joyous, part of a good community.

There were several things going on in the Glide ritual. Freedom for minorities and social justice for all were prominent themes. There were democratic signs in the ritual itself—e.g., the pastor remained on the same level as the parishioners while giving the sermon. The service was not an escape from daily life: the banners, song lyrics, and sermons all related to the struggle taking place outside. Above all, however, the ritual emotionally involved people and tried to be a celebration of life.

There was, then, something of a revolution in church rituals during the sixties. On the one hand, rituals changed to express democratic values. Even though the "celebration" at Glide Church was not an interaction ritual, freedom was proclaimed on the banners and the slides, as well as in the songs and the sermon. On the other hand, the new rituals were attempts to create new communal experiences that were expressive, pleasurable, and festive. It was the latter aspect that was dominant in ritual renewal within liberal Christianity.

The democratization of ritual has not spread widely. A study in the late 1970s of rituals at more than one hundred churches concluded that interaction-type rituals were, at best, rare. For example, in only two of 112 churches did lay people usually give a sermon (Tamney 1984:64). It may be that approximations to the interaction type are more common outside formal churches. Beginning in the seventies, 'house churches' began to appear. Shared participation in decision-making is characteristic of such groups, whose members avoid elaborate organization (Banks 1985).

Ritual renewal is real. The church rituals of the past, outside the Pentecostal movement, tended to be more authoritarian than free—more solemn, if not boring, than festive. Ducey suggested that the essence of these changes was to increase freedom. To some extent this is true. However, the dominant motive for ritual change has not been the desire to be free. More important than the desire for freedom as a source of inspiration for change has been a desire for celebration and community: "A vision for community is capturing the hopes and imaginations of many Christians in the last decades of the twentieth century" (Harder 1985:114). There is no necessary contradiction between having community and freedom. The former, however, does not require the latter. A sense of community can occur within a traditional ritual or a charismatic ritual, or an interaction ritual. The point is that community can be created in a variety of ways, most of which are not democratic. As long as people are mainly concerned about achieving community, the attainment of freedom is jeopardized.

Describing the ideal parish, an Episcopalian priest included a commitment to mutual ministry by clergy and laity, which would mean lay participation not only "in the act of worship itself but in the planning as well," but then he added: "as far as this is appropriate and possible" (Fenhagen 1977:17). All in all, Fenhagen's ideal parish has some resemblance to Ducey's interactive church. In Fenhagen's experience, however, laity were not very enthusiastic about the idea of mutual ministry. A major reason is that laity like "to feel cared for and secure at the expense of feeling slightly inferior and with less power" (Fenhagen 1977:25). Based on his experience and observation, Fenhagen is saying that people are willing to trade a sense of powerlessness for feelings of security and being cared for. Once again, we find evidence of the dominance of the need for community in religious matters.

In summary, over the past thirty years, ritual renewal has taken place within American Christianity, and in part this has been an attempt to empower the laity. The accommodation of liberal values, however, has been limited for several reasons. To begin with, *freedom* has various meanings—notably individual self-sufficiency, spontaneity, and democracy. The first meaning, of course, is incompatible with the existence of a church. In responding to libertarian aspirations, some churches have increased spontaneity, while others have democratized. The organizational preference for one or the other mode of libertarianism narrows the appeal of all groups. Moreover, the greater importance of community compared to freedom in the minds of people when they go to church makes religious accommodation of libertarianism less necessary and therefore less likely.

Self-Realization and Liberal Christianity

Christians have developed the Shakertown Pledge, which is a set of principles for simple living, the first four of which are:

- I declare myself to be a world citizen.

- I commit myself to lead an ecologically sound life.

- I commit myself to lead a life of creative simplicity and to share my personal wealth with the world's poor.

- I commit myself to join with others in reshaping institutions in order to bring about a more just global society in which each person has full access to the needed resources for her/his physical, emotional, intellectual, and spiritual growth (Fenhagen 1977:138).

This pledge, formulated in 1974, was motivated by a realization that we are foolishly wasting scarce natural resources, by an ethical conviction that the affluent should help the poor, and by a desire to live in a way that allows more attention to the spiritual side of life. In addition, the fourth point in the pledge includes the goal of personal growth in all its facets.

Compare the Shakertown Pledge to the criteria used by the Simple Living Collective of San Francisco.

- Does what I own or buy promote activity, self-reliance, and involvement, or does it induce passivity and dependence?

- Are my consumption patterns basically satisfying, or do I buy much that serves no real need?

- How tied is my present job and lifestyle to installment payments, maintenance and repair costs, and the expectations of others?

- Do I consider the impact of my consumption patterns on other people and on the earth? (Elgin 1981:66)

These criteria, in effect, justify simplicity in the name of freedom and self-realization. The Shakertown groups, on the other hand, subordinate self-concerns to ethical obligations such as to help the poor. Before mentioning personal growth, the Shakertown Pledge refers to being a world citizen, the need for an ecologically sound life, sharing wealth with the poor, and a just society.

James Fenhagen, an Episcopalian priest and a seminary dean, listed seven criteria to be used in evaluating a church congregation, the first three of which are:

1. Life is enhanced when a congregation takes seriously the communication of its biblical and theological tradition.

2. Life is enhanced when a congregation works at building and sustaining authentic community.

3. A critical sign of life for a congregation today would be the capacity to help people take upon themselves the discipline necessary for authentic personal and spiritual growth (Fenhagen 1977:9–11).

The order is important: first is the commitment to a religious tradition, then the effort to create unity, and third the encouragement of personal growth. Christians accept the pursuit of self-realization, but it is in the context of a prior commitment to a tradition and to a community. This is evident in the Shakertown Pledge and Fenhagen's criteria.

Don Browning (1987) has discussed in some detail the relation between Christian thought and various new psychologies. I shall consider only what he wrote about the humanistic psychologists who emphasize the importance of self-actualization.

The basic criticism Browning made of psychologists such as Abraham Maslow concerned the importance attributed to self-actualization. The belief that self-actualization is good in itself implies that all natural human capabilities are valuable, or at least acceptable, and thus worthy of being developed to their full potential. Browning (1987:83) objected to this implicit dismissal of the idea of a sinful human nature. He argued that, as an ethical system, humanistic psychology is not very useful because of its overly simplistic assumptions. For example, Carl Rogers believed that individuals who seek to actualize their potential learn that "doing what 'feels right' proves to be a competent and trustworthy guide to behavior which is truly satisfying." About this Browning wrote: "It is clear that Rogers is here presenting the idea that what is 'satisfying' to our basic need to actualize our own potentials is a trustworthy general procedure in all decision-making, even moral decisions" (Browning 1987:69). To help in understanding the ethical inadequacy of humanistic psychology from a Christian viewpoint, I shall summarize Maslow's ideas about morality, then return to Browning's criticism of humanistic psychology.

Self-Actualization and Selfishness

Maslow's link between self-actualization and morality was the mystical experience. He referred to moments of intense inner oneness accompanied by a simultaneous sense of oneness with the world as peak experiences. Increasingly, the frequency of such experiences became the goal of Maslow's movement. We were to develop ourselves fully and experience complete unity with the universe, the "unitive consciousness." Maslow believed that his own movement was itself transitional. He wrote: "I consider Humanistic, Third Force Psychology to be…a preparation for a still 'higher' Fourth Psychology, transpersonal, centered in the cosmos rather than in human needs and interests, going beyond humanness, identity, self-actualization, and the like" (1968:IV). In one of his last papers, "Theory Z," Maslow (1971:281) distinguished self-actualizers and transcenders. Transcendence, the experience of "unitive consciousness," became the sign of full humanness. To develop oneself came to mean to transcend the self. The ultimate step in developing the self was attaining an experience in which the boundary between self and other did not exist. The residue of this experience was a sense of union with others, so that self-actualization became all-actualization. For a transcender, love is spontaneous. Thus, having peak experiences linked together self-development and love.

In the counterculture, experiences of oneness were considered the experiential basis for a new morality of love.

> In every situation arising in life, one must determine what is the loving thing to do in that situation, in that moment, and then do it.... Whatever action is loving and actualizes and enhances the personhood of others is the proper action in that situation (Flowers 1984:17–18).

This hippie version of situational ethics reduced moral maxims to a single proposition: love everyone everywhere. Hippie morality was based on the experience of unity, which naturally would give rise to altruistic behavior.

Maslow's basic argument that personal development naturally involves caring is also a major premise of the New Age movement (Ferguson 1980:90–100). The fully developed person eschews a competition that means harming others and acts on the basis of a sense of union with others. In the New Age movement, the twin goals of self-development and community are bonded.

Browning's Critique

Christian commentators do not deny that mystical experiences can produce altruistic behavior. However, they question whether people's lives can become morally ordered simply as a result of experiences of wholeness.

Despite his psychological training, Maslow's view of personality seems naive. The state of complete personal development is supposedly characterized by inner unity. In the healthy person: "The conclusions of rational, careful thinking are apt to come to the same conclusions as those of the blind appetites. What such a person wants and enjoys is apt to be just what is good for him" (Maslow 1968:208). In another place, Maslow wrote that what he called the peak experience produces personal wholeness: "Now what I have been describing here may be seen as fusion of ego, id, superego, and ego-ideal, of conscious, preconscious, and unconscious, of primary and secondary processes, a synthesizing of pleasure principle with reality principle, a healthy regression without fear in the service of the greatest maturity, a true integration of the person at all levels" (Maslow 1968:96).

For Browning, this was just too simple:

In this [i.e., humanistic psychological] literature there is the remarkable implication that, when all people are fully aware of their own organismic needs and completely attuned to their own valuing processes, an almost pre-established harmony of wants and desires will reign over society and conflict will be at a minimum if it does not altogether disappear (Browning 1987:68–69).

Besides assuming the possibility of inner harmony, the humanistic psychologists assume the possibility of social harmony, and thus offer no rules for resolving interpersonal conflict.

This view postulates that the actualization of all potentialities is basically complementary, that differing potentialities can never really conflict, and that, for this reason, all people can pursue their own interests without fear that they will conflict with or be extinguished by the interests of other people. It is only if such a set of assumptions can be justified that it would be possible to live a life of uninhibited self-actualization without the threat of perpetual self-contradiction and continuous interpersonal and social conflict (Browning 1987:75).

In Maslow's optimistic version of psychology, people naturally pursue spiritual values and this entails no necessary conflict with physical drives, self-interest, or society. Yet, in one of his earlier writings, Maslow (1968:112) had written: "Intrinsic and necessary to the concept of self-actualization is a certain selfishness and self-protectiveness, a certain promise of necessary violence, even of ferocity." In his later work, Maslow's concern for wholeness seems, as Browning said, to have produced an oversimplified, convenient model of the person.

Thus, Browning believed that the counterculture was based on unacceptable assumptions. In his view, social order requires shared adherence to a set of values and ideals that form a basis for resolving conflicts and arranging priorities—i.e., social order requires an ethical code such as Christian ethics.

It is interesting, in light of this, that Browning (1987:65) also acknowledged that humanistic psychology has positively influenced Christianity. Many theologians, including liberal ones influenced by writers such as Reinhold Niebuhr, had believed that self-love was the major problem of our time. However, people such as Erich Fromm and Carl Rogers have convinced many theologians that an absence of a sense of self-worth is a more widespread problem. The humanistic psychologists have forced theologians to reassess the relation between self-love and love of neighbor.

It is entirely possible to argue that Niebuhr and other Protestant theologians do not make enough out of the problem of self-hate and the loss of self-esteem in their analysis of the human condition. This is indeed arguable. It is, in fact, probably the case.... But to acknowledge this should not obscure the truth that original sin is the profounder problem. For it is the problem left over when relative health has been achieved (Browning 1987:144).

The humanistic psychologists have also affected the theological understanding of love. Especially in Protestant circles, love was primarily associated with self-sacrifice. Niebuhr wrote: "Christ as the norm of human nature defines the final perfection of man in history.... It is the perfection of sacrificial love" (quoted in Browning 1987:145). In recent times, another interpretation of love, closer to Catholic and biblical sources, has gained prominence among liberal theologians generally. Central to this latter view is the idea of equal regard—i.e., one should have equal regard for self and others.

Put simply, the modern psychologies, especially the humanistic psychologies, have put pressure on the culture as a whole and theology in particular to build a greater place for self-regard into their models of human fulfillment (Browning 1987:156).

In sum, over the last fifty years or so, the value of self-actualization has become increasingly influential within liberal Christianity. Especially important for my analysis, Christian ethicists have accommodated to the relatively new cultural valuing of self-realization by developing the ethical principle of equal regard for self and other.[1] However, Christian thinkers have tended to subordinate self-actualization to achieving community and to meeting ethical obligations. This is implied in the Shakertown Pledge and Fenhagen's criteria and made clear in Browning's analysis of humanistic psychology. Theologically, a belief that human nature is sinful is incompatible with primacy being given to self-actualization. Moreover, Browning denied the adequacy of a natural morality based on peak experiences. He affirmed the necessity of some ethical code that would transcend immediate personal interests in controlling human behavior.

The Affluence Ethic and Liberal Christianity

I shall only illustrate a general point, namely that liberal Christianity has come to accept a morally neutral, pleasure-centered part of living. My illustration concerns food. Riesman (1961:145) pointed out that, after World War II, middle-class culture increasingly valued for its pleasure not only sexual intercourse but also eating. The attitude toward food is a useful indicator of a more general attitude toward material pleasure.

Jeff Smith, a Methodist minister and chef, is the star of "The Frugal Gourmet" on public television. He travels the country speaking about "food as sacrament and celebration." He has pointed out that religious thinkers have tended to believe that gastronomic pleasure is a sin of the flesh. "It's the Puritan influence—they refused to let us have fun at the table" (quoted in Hassell 1986:8). Smith himself wants to tie together food and spiritual issues, which he does in part by emphasizing the solidarity-building consequence of the feasting ritual. But the important point is that Smith's comments illustrate the liberal Christian acceptance of sensual pleasure as a goal in and of itself.

In the course of discussing the merits of fasting, other Christian writers have taken the time to praise good eating. In *Fasting Reconsidered*, the author commented: "The Christian who feels guilty when she enjoys a glass of good red wine...is not a good Christian" (Ryan 1981:12). And: "Certainly eating is meant to be one of life's chief joys...." (Ryan 1981:145). While less enthusiastic about eating, Morton Kelsey (1972:185) was careful to separate fasting from the rejection of pleasure: "The fact that one fasts certainly does not mean that they cannot enjoy a good meal."

I shall not document it, but having personally experienced a change in attitude toward sexual pleasure on the part of Catholic priests, from silence to open encouragement of the laity, I know that attitudes have changed not just concerning the joy of eating.

The new attitudes imply an acceptance of pleasure pure and simple. This change means a willingness, intended or not, to allow values not considered religious to govern behavior in certain contexts. That is to say, this change allows choices to be made on the basis of seeking to maximize pleasure, which has not been linked with salvation. One consequence of modernization, then, is the enlargement of the acceptable zone of life that is ethically neutral, in which values not traditionally religious may hold sway. This elevation of non-moral criteria, especially aesthetic ones, is a crucial part of the counterculture. The question is, how large will religion allow this zone to become?

There is an inevitable uneasiness built into accommodating the affluence ethic.

Conclusion

As discussed in the Introduction, some degree of secularization
seems an inevitable consequence of modernization. However, the
extent to which a religion loses significance in part depends on its
accommodation to modern ideas. In this chapter, it has been shown
that Christianity has more or less accommodated the counterculture—i.e., the mix of the alternative tradition, libertarianism, the self-
realization ethos, and the affluence ethic.

The Jesus movement, charismatic Christianity, and the renewed
interest in mysticism accommodated Christianity to the alternative
tradition. However, Christian accommodation to this tradition is limited by the priority given to the Bible and ethical codes over either
personal religious experience or magic, and by the historically recent
accommodation to libertarianism, which conflicts with the emphasis
on charismatic authority in the alternative tradition.

Regarding libertarianism, Westerners have accumulated quite
different connotations of freedom: independence, spontaneity, and
participatory democracy. The ideal of the completely independent
person is, of course, incompatible with the existence of a church.
Moreover, although hypothetically possible, it is doubtful whether
any church can endure that models itself on groups such as the Diggers. The requirements to survive as a church probably preclude a
religious version of radical libertarian organization becoming available for any significant number of people.

Christianity, although mostly within the Protestant churches,
has by now a long tradition of accommodating to less radical forms of
libertarianism. Yet there are limits on this process as well. No institution can simultaneously provide spontaneity and participatory
democracy. The charismatic movement attracted many people interested in more spontaneous, expressive rituals, whereas in the liberal
churches developments such as the use of interaction rituals no doubt
appealed to those who favored participatory democracy. Theoretically, over time a religion might provide individuals with both types of
experience; this would have to be a very flexible group, and I am not
aware of any real examples. It seems more likely that religious groups
will tend to offer just one, if any, form of freedom. Thus, the diverse
meanings of freedom will produce diverse religious groups, thereby
limiting the potential popularity of any one group.

However, people are not putting pressure on religious leaders to increase freedom within the churches. When Americans go to religious services, they are more in search of a sense of community than of freedom. The demand for church freedom is not high; the relative neglect of freedom, however, can be subtly disturbing for modern people.

Finally, even when religious leaders seek to increase freedom, the effect of their initiatives may be the opposite of what was intended. To oversimplify, we can think of new rituals being either charismatic or interactional. The former is more popular. I take this to mean, in part, that spontaneity is more important than democracy when contemporary people seek freer ritual forms. However, spontaneous events are open to evolving into authoritarian situations by being dominated by charismatic individuals.

I suggest that people are turning to churches more for community than for freedom—and more out of an interest in spontaneity than in democracy—because churches play a secondary, compensatory role in modern society. In other words, the role assigned the church in society is not to act as the vanguard but as the place of escape from the frustrations caused by public institutions that seem alien and often threatening. In modern societies, the economic institution is dominant; as long as this institution is exploitative and bureaucratic in nature, churches will be expected to provide experiences of community and celebration. In addition, urbanization increases feelings of isolation and aloneness. Because public life in a modern society is so alienating and joyless, people turn to religion for magic, emotional release, communal oneness, and the experience of celebration. Thus, contemporary Christianity has accommodated more to the alternative tradition than to libertarianism. Being spontaneous, we feel more real; being in a community, we feel more whole.

Liberal Christianity is also accommodating the relatively new aspects of the counterculture by accepting the value of self-realization and by going along with an enlarging of the religious neutral zone of living.

Again, however, there are limits to this process. Consider the valuing of self-realization. I just discussed how church members seem willing to sacrifice libertarian goals for a sense of community. The same analysis can be made substituting self-realization for freedom. In the contemporary world, specific churches are valued more as places providing experiences of community than as places of opportunity for self-exploration and personal growth. Thus, dropping out of a church has been frequently explained by a lack of warmth and friendliness in the churches to which the dropouts had belonged (Hoge and Roozen 1979:64–67). Moreover, giving greater priority to building community than to personal growth (except in the sense of ceasing to be a sinner) is built into Christian theology. Thus, the association of Christianity and community, while in part a result of the secondary social role of churches, is also mandated by the Christian theological tradition.

In addition, there are philosophical limits on the extent to which liberal Christianity can value self-realization. Some theologians now recognize a moral obligation to develop oneself, but this is tempered by the belief in sinful human nature. Moreover, theologians believe that inner and social conflict are unavoidable; thus, a peaceful existence requires commitment to a moral code that will inevitably cause some frustration and self-denial.

Similarly, while liberal Christianity can accommodate the affluence ethic by accepting an enlargement of the religious neutral zone of living, the priority of ethics over aesthetic criteria inherently limits the Christian accommodation.

This analysis has obvious implications for religious popularity. If my model is correct, the fundamentalist accommodation of the alternative tradition strengthens this branch of Christianity. At the same time, the liberal accommodation to the counterculture should aid its survival into the future. However, as in the case of socialism, a full accommodation between liberal Christianity and the counterculture is not possible. There are limits to this accommodation. Thus, even liberal Christianity will have a weakened role in future society.[2]

❖ 5

The Popularity of the Christian Right

Just as the sixties was the decade of the counterculture, the seventies and eighties seemed to belong to this culture's opponents. During the seventies, some 25 "culturally-defensive religious movements" formed that focused on abortion, public prayer, gender roles, and the like (Wuthnow 1986:19). The targets included expressions of the alternative tradition such as the infamous cults, radical libertarian ideas such as free love, and especially the declared decline in puritanical morality as supposedly evidenced in new levels of selfishness and materialism. Most of these defensive movements were associated with fundamentalist Christianity.

Although the emergence of the counterculture was the spark that ignited the political activism of the fundamentalists, their dissatisfaction with modern society had been smoldering throughout the century. This branch of Christianity is an example of what was called "traditionalist religion" in the Introduction. Fundamentalism, then, is much more than a rejection of the counterculture. It is a defensive movement in response to modernity.

The obvious question is: Why do traditionalist religions exist in modern society? Or, more specifically: Why are Americans going to fundamentalist churches? One reason, of course, is because members of fundamentalist churches have larger families than members of liberal churches (Roof and McKinney 1987:161). Such a demographic analysis is important yet insufficient. The obvious question remains: Why don't all these children flee to other churches?

In this chapter, after briefly describing the nature of fundamentalism, I will make the point that in fact fundamentalism has accommodated modernity to a significant extent. Thus, its popularity is not as mysterious as it seems at first glance. However, some fundamentalists belong to the Christian Right, a segment of fundamentalism which *does* struggle against certain aspects of modernity. The theoretical framework proposed in the Introduction does not explain the appeal of the Christian Right. A major part of this chapter, therefore, concerns why a Christian Right movement gained support in the

United States. Finally, just as in past chapters I have considered what limits the popularity of liberal religions, so this chapter ends with a discussion of what limits the appeal of the Christian Right.

In this chapter, then, I will discuss: (1) the nature of fundamentalism; (2) its accommodation to modernization; (3) the distinguishing characteristics of the Christian Right; (4) why the Right appeals to some modern people; and (5) why such appeal is limited.

What Is Fundamentalism?

In the United States, fundamentalism is the name given to a religious movement which originated within American Protestantism in the early part of this century. It was a transdenominational protest by diverse groups "united by their fierce opposition to modernist attempts to bring Christianity into line with modern thought" (Marsden 1982:4).

In terms of the discussion of secularization in the Introduction, perhaps the critical idea distinguishing liberal and fundamentalist Christians is desacralization. Whereas liberals tend to accept an expanding zone of religiously neutral activity, fundamentalists tend to oppose this social change. They believe the Bible is a sure guide to living and form a constituency committed to using the Bible as the only foundation for living. Thus, fundamentalists resist desacralization.

It is important, therefore, that the Bible be interpreted clearly and confidently. Thus, the most basic belief of fundamentalism is that every word in the Bible is true (Richardson and Bowden 1983:223). Those who agree with this statement, however, are not necessarily all saying the same thing. For instance, while some fundamentalists believe in the literal truth of every line in whatever Bible they have in their homes, others believe in the literal truth only of the original, lost version of the Bible. Generally, however, fundamentalists believe the Bible must be taken literally, although not necessarily every word in it, and thus reject the liberal idea that the nature of a religion changes over time.

Believing that there is a clear Biblical teaching, fundamentalists give primacy to religious scripture in all matters. They do not accept a separate secular realm of thought or action. All of life is to be interpreted in light of doctrine; ideally, all events are read through the Bible (Burton, Johnson, and Tamney 1989:345). For instance, when a tornado unexpectedly struck their region, members of a fundamentalist church tried to discern the religious meaning of this disaster. They proposed various interpretations, agreeing on none of them. "The only intolerable possibility was that the whole thing was 'merely natural'" (Ammerman 1987:71).

Just as the primacy of the Bible is the positive basis of fundamentalism, so distrust of human designs to remake the world is its
negative basis. Fundamentalists hold an image of humans as sinful
and prone to arrogance. They decry what they perceive as rampant
"selfism." Paul Vitz's (1977) *Psychology as Religion* has as a subtitle
"The Cult of Self-Worship," which more precisely than the book's title
conveys Vitz's intention. Although a Roman Catholic, Vitz wrote his
book as an expression of conservative Christianity. He argued that
self-actualization theory functions as a religion—i.e., it furnishes people with a set of principles about how to live and with an object of
devotion, the self. Vitz used the term *selfism* "to refer to this religion
and its rationale for self-expression, creativity, and the like" (Vitz
1977:37). Vitz's alternative view derives from "the Christian injunc-
tion to *lose* the self" (91). The Christian perspective, according to Vitz,
emphasizes duty and obligation. "We need sermons on radical obedience, on the mysticism of submissive surrender of the will, on the
beauty of dependency, on how to find humility" (129). In one fundamentalist church, "the formula was J–O–Y: Jesus first, Others second,
Yourself last" (Ammerman 1987:90).

Thus, fundamentalists strongly challenge what they identify as
the core of modernism—i.e., secular humanism. As depicted by fundamentalists, this ideology is atheistic and expresses confidence in
humanity's ability to determine its own destiny through the use of
reason and science (Smith 1985:40). Although probably few Americans espouse secular humanism as just described, this portrait of evil
helps us understand the nature of fundamentalism.

In sum, fundamentalism is a world view that makes the Bible
the basis of life and discourages purely human efforts to create a better world. More specifically, fundamentalism means believing that: (1)
the Bible is to be taken literally; (2) life and interpretations of life must
be understood and evaluated in terms of Biblical statements; (3)
human nature is sinful; and (4) selfism and secular humanism are
important contemporary evils. Implicit in this world view is a rejection that secularism has any place in the world, a faith that desacralization can be eliminated, and a belief that only when all people are
fully committed to Jesus Christ will there be reason to be optimistic
about the future.

The Appeal of Fundamentalism

In light of the ideas elaborated on in the preceding chapter, the
appeal of fundamentalism is not surprising. Two ideas that emerged

from a consideration of the counterculture were that religious popularity is enhanced by accommodating the alternative tradition and by
providing community. As to the first point, it is mainly the Pentecostal churches within fundamentalism that have accommodated the
alternative tradition. Regarding community, evidence suggests that
this reward is experienced more often in fundamentalist churches. For
example, such churches retain as members a higher percentage of
children born to church members. Moreover, given the same level of
potential religious dissatisfaction, Americans raised in fundamentalist
churches are more likely to remain Christians than those raised as
members of mainstream churches (Tamney, Powell, and Johnson
1989:227). Such evidence suggests that fundamentalist churches, more
than others, have more effectively evoked commitment and community among members of congregations (Kelley 1978; Roof and McKinney 1987:183). This is not hard to believe, especially in congregations
that are charismatic or involve members in each other's lives through
the public sharing of personal testimonials. Overall, then, given my
theory of religious popularity, the continued appeal of fundamentalism is not surprising.

But I want to go further and argue that it is an oversimplifica-
tion to describe fundamentalism as anti-modern in the sociological
sense. In the Introduction, the relatively irreversible aspects of modernization were listed as: technological development, scientific
progress, structural differentiation, cultural pluralism, cultural differentiation, and the four modern ideational sets. Regarding the first
three aspects, fundamentalists are not in opposition to them. Regarding cultural pluralism and cultural differentiation, fundamentalists
are reluctant to admit these traits are of any intrinsic value, but they
recognize that accommodation to them may be a political necessity. In
these matters, the difference between fundamentalist and liberal
Christians is more a matter of degree than of kind. Even in regard to
modern ideas, fundamentalists have made some accommodation.
Given the importance of the ideational sets in my analysis, I will consider their relationships to fundamentalism in a little more detail, and
in each case show the nature of the accommodation.

Fundamentalism and Libertarianism

One segment of fundamentalists see themselves as descendants
of the early Baptists who were part of the radical religious movement
that accompanied the English revolution in the seventeenth century.
Like their predecessors the Anabaptists, the Baptists stood for the separation of church and state, for liberty of conscience, and for religious

tolerance. Basic to their outlook was a commitment to "soul liberty." Each person is accountable to God and responsible for interpreting the scripture as well as for applying it to her or his life. Each Baptist congregation was independent of the others—i.e., the denomination did not control a local church. Rather, congregations were governed by lay elders who were elected by the congregation. The Baptists "were able to create a system of democratic, representative assemblies with no previous parallel, at least in English history" (McGregor 1986:34).

This is not to say that these churches were ideal democracies. For example, on doctrinal matters each congregation sought consensus, which method allowed no room for principled dissent, so dissenters were often expelled (McGregor 1986:40). Although the Baptists were not originally (as they are not now) proponents of total libertarianism as that set of ideas is now understood, it must be accepted that the early Baptists were an important part of the libertarian revolution. Of course, then as now, not all seemingly democratic churches are that way in practice. Yet, to this day some fundamentalist churches are among the most democratic within Christendom.

Fundamentalism and Socialism

Fundamentalists have never embraced socialist ideology as developed on the continent. But then few Americans of any religious persuasion have. However, fundamentalism does have roots in the nineteenth-century evangelical movement, which included many social reformers. Thus, recent research has found that, among white Protestants, fundamentalists more than others supported economic restructuring. For example, fundamentalists more than other Protestants tended to agree that the government should take steps to reduce the income differences between the rich and the poor such as by raising the taxes of the wealthy or by giving income assistance to the poor (Tamney, Burton, and Johnson 1989). Illustrative of a more conservative approach to social justice, the M.B.A. program at Eastern College in Pennsylvania prepares students to be entrepreneurs for Biblical justice. According to a brochure, students in the program are "to become a new breed of Christian revolutionaries who can make a lasting difference in the world by helping to establish economic justice for the poor."

To this day, then, fundamentalists tend to favor social policies that are meant to achieve social justice. So, although it is true that fundamentalists are not socialist supporters, it is also true that within this religious movement there has been, and continues to be, support for programs meant to achieve the basic socialist goal of social justice (Tamney, Burton, and Johnson 1989).

Fundamentalism and the Counterculture

Even regarding countercultural ideas, there has been some accommodation on the part of fundamentalism. Inner-worldly asceticism is an integral part of the fundamentalist legacy. Such asceticism is wary of worldly pleasure, especially if it is spontaneous or done "without care," and emphasizes the need to control and deny the self (Hunter 1987:50–51). Hunter has reviewed the evidence that suggests that, although fundamentalists were inner-worldly ascetics in the past, this is less true today. Moral condemnation of such activities as dancing and going to the movies has declined significantly since mid-century. Fundamentalist marriage manuals now accept and applaud recreational reasons for intercourse and give information on how to maximize sexual pleasure (Lewis and Brissert 1986).

Similar changes have occurred with regard to the self. Hunter (1987:69–70) listed a number of Christian books that convey the message that developing one's potential is what God wants us to do. A recent study examined the relation between holding fundamentalist beliefs and accepting the self-actualization ideology and found no relation: fundamentalists were as likely as others to accept this ideology (Tamney and Johnson 1989). However, the study also suggested that self-actualization meant different things to fundamentalists than to non-fundamentalists. Some sense of what this means is conveyed by the following statement made by a Methodist student at an evangelical college; she might not have held fundamentalists beliefs, but her comment illustrates how self-development can be linked to traditional duties.

> To me, self-fulfillment is very important. Getting married and having kids would be a big part of that; so would finding a good job. Ultimately, though, my fulfillment would come through my belief in God (quoted in Hunter 1987:67).

When fundamentalists accommodate to countercultural elements, they reinterpret certain traits of this ideational set so as to fit them into their traditional religious framework. Thus, while I believe it true that fundamentalism is trying to adapt to such aspects of the counterculture as the belief in self-actualization and the affluence ethic, it also seems true that such accommodation is less than that which is occurring among religious liberals.

In summary, fundamentalists accept modern society even to the point of accommodating the modern ideational sets. Admittedly, this accommodation seems less than what characterizes liberal Christianity. The interplay of a fundamentalist's desire to base life on the Bible and the recognition that modern ideas have some value is not fully understood. Yet, fundamentalism clearly cannot be described as anti-modern.

But, fundamentalism can be subdivided into those who have relatively speaking accommodated modernity and those who have more staunchly resisted modernity (the Christian Right).[1] On the face of it, my theoretical framework would seem unable to explain why the Christian Right movement exists in a modern society. The remainder of this chapter is devoted to understanding this movement. Therefore, I will describe the Christian Right within fundamentalism and explain its appeal. I will then discuss the forces limiting the popularity of the Christian Right.

The Christian Right

The Christian Right is a political movement whose program is religious. The major organization within this movement during the 1980s was Moral Majority, Incorporated. Jerry Falwell, while leader of the Moral Majority, said to his fellow ministers:

> What can you do from the pulpit? You can register people to vote. You can explain the issues to them. And you can endorse candidates, right there in church on Sunday morning (quoted in Guth 1983:37).

Ministers risk losing the tax exempt status for their churches if they clearly endorse a candidate "on Sunday morning," but ministers have found ways to express their preferences such as by using moral scorecards to evaluate opposing candidates. Some religious leaders, such as Pat Robertson, have run for public office. The Christian Right, then, is a political movement led by preachers from fundamentalist Protestantism.

Certain distinguishing aspects of the Christian Right would, according to my framework, add to its popularity. First, unlike other Christians, evangelicals included, the Right portrays the United States as the new chosen people whose destiny it is to save the world. Falwell said: "God has raised up America in these last days for the cause of world evangelization and for the protection of his people, the Jews" (quoted in Christianity Today 1981:1098). The linking of religion and national identity would gain support from some highly patriotic Christians, although the linkage no doubt would displease others. A second distinguishing characteristic of the Christian Right is the leadership's religious legitimation of capitalism. Quoting Jerry Falwell again: "The free-enterprise system is clearly outlined in the Book of Proverbs in the Bible.... Ownership of property is biblical. Ambitious and successful business management is clearly outlined as part of God's plan for His people" (Falwell 1980:13). Given that many Americans believe in capitalism, which they associate with libertarianism, they would find the presentation of free enterprise as God's preferred economic system attractive.

Other distinguishing characteristics of the Christian Right, however, would seem to turn many people away because they are clearly anti-modern. The Christian Right is that part of Christianity that generally resists the cultural aspects of modernization, including cultural pluralism, cultural differentiation, and the modern ideational sets. Regarding modern ideas, the Christian Right rejects socialist values and gives an unqualified endorsement to capitalism. Its rejection of the counterculture is quite severe; one Rightist described the New Age as a manifestation of barbarism (Cumbey 1983). In what follows, I will briefly discuss an aspect of the Right's anti-libertarianism —namely its desire to have a state-enforced morality—then its critique of cultural pluralism, and finally its efforts to overcome cultural differentiation. After describing these aspects of the Right, I shall return to the topic of its popular appeal.

Church-State Relationship

Liberals tend to affirm the institutionally differentiated society. They accept the separation of church and state. This is less true of fundamentalists in general (Tamney and Johnson 1987) and not at all true of Christian Right leaders.

Unlike many fundamentalists, members of the Christian Right *in effect* are trying to increase church-state entanglement. They seek support for religion in general rather than the establishment of a specific religious organization. The Christian Right argues that state support for "religion in general" is constitutional. Among Rightists "religion in general" means acceptance of the Christian God and the Bible as the word of God. Thus, the Christian Right disowns state support for any particular creed or denomination, but seeks the establishment of a basic Christianity (Hill and Owen 1982:45–46).

The Critique of Pluralism

Implied in their attitude toward the state is the Right's opposition to pluralism, which exists to various degrees. An example of Christian

Right thinking is the statement by Joseph Sobran. In his opinion, the authors of the Constitution meant by "religion" only the various forms of Christianity known to them and not the variety of religions known to the modern anthropologist. Religious freedom should be understood as the right to worship the Judeo-Christian God. As Sobran wrote: "Belief in the God of our fathers is central to the American tradition. Pluralism is an adjunct of this belief, not a substitute for it" (Sobran 1986:14). For the Christian Right, pluralism is acceptable only to the extent religions fit their notion of basic Christianity.

A more emotional, broader rightist perspective is presented in Constance Cumbey's (1983) *The Hidden Dangers of the Rainbow*, which is subtitled "The New Age Movement and Our Coming Age of Barbarism." Her book was said to be one of the most influential books that has brought the New Age movement to the attention of Christians (Burrows 1986:17). What I want to emphasize, however, is not Cumbey's treatment of the New Age movement but of religions other than her own fundamentalist Christianity. Cumbey criticized religions other than Judaism and Christianity, as well as those individuals sympathetic to such religions.

> While there are certain superficial similarities among most religions, orthodox Judaism and Christianity stand in direct opposition to every other belief system. It is safe to say, however, that nearly all non–Judeo-Christian religions are extremely similar because, as the Bible indicates, they come from one source, the 'god of this world' —Satan himself (Cumbey 1983:89).

Cumbey criticized Father Theodore Hesburgh, then of the University of Notre Dame, because of his ecumenical interest in non–Judeo-Christian religions (151). Pluralism and ecumenism were identified with Satan (39).

Cumbey wrote: "The heart of the New Age movement is old-fashioned Hindu occultism, which embodies the ancient lie of the serpent right out of the Garden of Eden" (168–169). In 1985, an organization called Campus Crusade for Christ organized a showing of the film "Gods of the New Age" at Ball State University. A student reviewer commented in the Ball State Daily News (24 January): "To associate all Hindu ideas and practices with evil seems to be an over-reaction by the well-meaning Christians involved in this film's production.... The film ended with scenes of Hitler and his army with hands raised, and the sounds of Hitler continued as the scene changed to dancing Hindu worshippers with their hands in the air."

The more restrained Sobran and the meaner Cumbey express aspects of the Christian Right mindset. In both examples, appreciation of other religions is rejected in favor of religious exclusivism. At the extreme represented by Cumbey, the enemy is distorted, misrepresented, and satanized—thereby eliminating any justification for sympathetic understanding.

Cultural Differentiation

The Christian Right seeks to insulate itself against modern culture. They have their own bookstores, magazines, cassettes, movies, radio shows, and television programs (Ammerman 1987:114–119). Ideally, the Right would be exposed only to those espousing its religiously integrated culture.

Although the Right cannot eliminate science and art, it seeks to co-opt these cultural realms. For example, the controversy over the teaching of evolution in schools expresses how the Religious Right relates to science. Briefly, Rightists believe God did not allow humans to evolve from lower species; rather, they affirm that God created, literally, the first humans. Rightists are trying to use scientific evidence to prove the sudden creation of the universe from nothing. What is more significant, however, is their establishment of their own scientific organizations. Going beyond the specific issue of evolution, these organizations express the Rightist approach to science. They believe that the Bible is without error. Thus, if the conclusions of scientists are clearly contrary to their understanding of the Bible, they conclude that the scientists have erred. To many scientists, the dogmatic attitude of those advocating creation-science means the destruction of the scientific spirit (Gieryn, Bevins, and Zehr 1985).

Their attitude toward science illustrates how the Christian Rightists relates to all nonreligious realms of intellectual activity. Intellectual pursuits autonomous of religious authority are to be eliminated.

The Christian Right, then, opposes the cultural aspects of modernization. Why, then, does the Christian Right exist? In what follows, I will give special attention to the Moral Majority Inc., an organization that was founded in 1979 by the Reverend Jerry Falwell. Both Falwell and his organization captured a great deal of media attention. It was the best-known organization expressing Christian Right values and beliefs during the 1980s. For 1986, the last year the Moral Majority as such existed, a reasonable estimate would be that between 12 and 20 percent of the American population were favorably disposed toward it (Tamney and Johnson 1988). The question, then, is: Why did the Christian Right in general, and the Moral Majority in particular, gain support in a modern society?

The Appeal of the Christian Right

To explain support for the Moral Majority, I will discuss three topics: the affinity between the Christian Right and political conservatism, the appeal of the Christian Right to authoritarian people, and the significance of traditional morality to modern people.

The Christian Right and Political Conservatism

There is no doubt that political conservatives played a significant role in the creation of the Christian Right (Reichley 1986). In 1976, conservatives launched a campaign to save the United States by making it a "Christian Republic." They were aided by Christian leaders associated with the fundamentalist organization, Campus Crusade for Christ. A basic belief of the campaign was that the free-enterprise system is the Christian economic system, and the goals included the abolishment of the minimum wage and reduction of the federal government's role in providing social services (Muncie Star 1976). In 1979, the leader of the Conservative Caucus, Howard Phillips, persuaded a Baptist preacher, Jerry Falwell, to form the Moral Majority (Pierard 1985:99).

By the late sixties, Richard Nixon and his advisers had decided to build a new majority based on "the traditional values of middle-class Americans—hard work, individual enterprise, orderly behavior, love of country, moral piety, and material progress" (Hodgson 1976:422). Since then, conservative political leaders have tried to use "social issues" to divide the Democrats and win over the Independents. What made individuals such as Jerry Falwell attractive to these Republicans was their ability to reach the working class through their television programs, the audiences for which grew in size during the seventies, and through their mass-mailing campaigns, which were based in part on the accumulation of addresses of the people responding to their television appeals.

Political conservatives supported the Christian Right, then, because they wanted to win support for their economic conservatism from voters whose economic self-interest had led them in the past to favor Democratic politics. But this is not the only link between political conservatives and the Christian Right.

Political Conservatism and the Church-State Relationship

Political conservatives are committed not only to capitalism but to a moral tradition. They believe that capitalism developed in the West because of the existence of a favorable moral climate. Understandably, then, conservatives want to preserve this moral milieu. Moreover, it is feared that unbridled freedom would lead to a war of all against all. Jeane Kirkpatrick, the former American ambassador to the United Nations, has emphasized the importance of sustaining an established moral code (Kirkpatrick 1982). The correct political line, according to Kirkpatrick, is to value tradition, to have schools that transform traditional values into ordinary habits, and to accept gradual change. Such a conservative approach is needed because humans are naturally prone to harming each other.

Kirkpatrick feared two things, idealism and individuality. The first offers unrealizable goals such as equality and justice, and the second leads to chaos. Being idealistic or valuing individuality are socially destructive because such attitudes do not assume the evilness of human nature.

> The notion of the 'natural' moral man turns out to be no more tenable than the notion that children learn best when left alone to motivate themselves. The natural savage is no more likely to observe, to learn, or to know the rules of democracy than the rules of baseball. He is as likely to swing the bat at the umpire as at the ball, as likely to fight as to vote. Teachers, lessons, and explanations are required to produce competent players and good citizens. Concepts like truth, honor, teamwork, responsibility, rule of law, restraint in use of power, and respect for others, must be introduced, illustrated, and transformed somehow into habits. In this process the roles of the school and the teacher are not only legitimate; they are irreducible and irreplaceable (Kirkpatrick 1982:244).

As already noted, Cumbey (1983) referred to the "coming age of barbarism," but this image of a possible future as barbaric is not unique to her. The British conservative member of Parliament, St. John-Stevas (1984:487), described contemporary society as threatened by "a new barbarism." This image expresses a conservative assessment of the countercultural revolution and motivates conservatives not only to support the old morality, but to accept a stronger role for the state in shoring up this morality.

The essence of this "new barbarism" is self-love or selfism. Such an attitude supposedly undermines the work ethic and threatens social order. Expressing this viewpoint, then–Attorney General of the United States Edwin Meese spoke of fearing the spread of a "cult of the self" and claimed that public schools were removing all references to traditional religion while replacing them with the "jargon and ritual and morality of the cult of the self" (quoted in Buie 1985:4). Conservatives perceived the rise of a "new barbarism," requiring an activist state to strengthen public endorsement of traditional values—i.e., values supportive of self-restraint, the work ethic, and free enterprise. Support for a state-religion alliance was expressed by a conservative Chief Justice of the U.S. Supreme Court, who wrote that "nothing…requires government to be strictly neutral between religion and irreligion, nor prohibits Congress or the states from pursuing legitimate secular ends through non-discriminating sectarian means" (Rehnquist 1985:13).

Social order requires religion. The implications of this conservative dictum were spelled out by William Bennett, while he was the Secretary of Education. State neutrality toward religion is bad policy because, Bennett suggested, it means "neutrality to those values that issue from religion" (Yoder 1985:7). Conservatives are critical of American public education because, in their view, public schools seek a value-free education (Curry and Riley 1986:155). Bennett spoke out in favor of indirect public aid for religious schools because they are freer to instill moral values. "Catholic schools, he said, can be unambiguous about their goals of instilling moral values, 'and that provides an advantage'" (Buie 1986:7). The conservative belief in the need for moral education, and more broadly for a shared public morality, has led conservatives to favor state support for religion.

The affinity between the Christian Right and political conservatism should now be clear. First, Christian Right leaders and political conservatives share a commitment to capitalism. Second, both groups identify selfism as a major evil of modern society, and both groups are eager to use the state to reinforce an anti-selfist, traditional morality. Thus, although the Christian Right was not state-supported, it did receive encouragement, advice, and favors from an important political faction, and this helps to explain its popularity.

Authoritarianism and the Christian Right

But why does the Christian Right appeal to those not committed to political conservatism? To expand our understanding of the appeal of the Christian Right, I will discuss the results of a series of research projects carried out by Stephen D. Johnson and myself in the Lynds' (1929) Middletown. Our goal was to find out why people supported the Moral Majority, and the work was done during the years 1981 through 1984, when Falwell's organization was the popular flagship of the Christian Right. (The results are summarized in Tamney and Johnson 1988.)

In our Middletown research, a measure of authoritarianism was found to be directly related to the Christian Right orientation (Johnson and Tamney 1985a:992). We suggested that authoritarianism was a personality basis for the appeal of the Christian Right.

> The authoritarians of America then seem to be a group of people who readily attend to right-wing, religious causes and serve as a foundation of support for the purposes of these causes. The need for a feeling of order in their lives and their tendency to condemn what they consider to be non-conformists...make authoritarians more susceptible to the preachings that there is a threatening group of liberal secularists who are trying to destroy their conventional, traditional way of life. The authoritarians' need to have authorities direct their lives makes them more likely to accept the authoritarian structure of many Christian Right churches, in which the minister *is* the church [Hill and Owen 1982:131], and to accept the ideological view of many Christian Right churches that God is the only sovereign or real authority over all persons and nations....

Wald, Owen, and Hill (1989b) denied that the Christian Right is an army of authoritarians. They distinguished authoritarianism—a type of personality characterized by a need to be domineering and a tendency for slavish dependency on authority figures—from what they called authority-mindedness. "To put it simply, authority-mindedness is an ideological commitment that values authoritativeness and obedience as a matter of principle rather than the outgrowth of a personality disorder" (Wald, Owen, and Hill 1989b:95). For example, a person with this outlook would agree that "There is only one right way to do anything" and that "A true Christian is absolutely certain what he or she believes." I do not believe their study adequately distinguishes authoritarianism and authority-mindedness, but it is worth noting that the researchers found that Christian Right supporters are more authority-minded than opponents.

Wald, Owen, and Hill argued that fundamentalists are expected to "surrender to the Lord," and fundamentalist pastors tend to expect unquestioned acceptance of their Biblical interpretation. Thus, fundamentalism is a form of religion that emphasizes the importance of accepting authority. Ammerman tied a preference for such a religion to the modern condition:

> As long as there is a modern world characterized by seeming chaos, there will be believers who react to that world by

refusing to grant it legitimacy. Although some may do so in soli-
tary reflection, most will seek out social structures in which cer-
tainty can take the place of doubt, in which clear rules and
authority can take the place of subjectivity, and in which truth is
truth without compromise (1987:212).

Ammerman studied a Christian Right congregation. Appropriately, her comments (as those of Wald, Owen, and Hill) better fit the
Christian Right branch of fundamentalism. Although it remains
unclear whether the preference for authoritarian religion is a consequence of personality or a societal condition, or both, the evidence
suggests that Christian Rightists are people who prefer a religion that
emphasizes obeying authority figures. Thus, it is suggested that there
are people who, in a time of change especially, prefer an anti-libertarian religion.

Social Traditionalism and the Christian Right

The Middletown project tried to determine what united Moral
Majoritarians. One possibility was that they were all committed to
capitalism. Moral Majority supporters, however, were not distinguished by their economic beliefs. Commitment to capitalism did
characterize the leadership and was the reason political conservatives
supported the Moral Majority, but the popular appeal of the Moral
Majority did not result from a shared commitment to free enterprise.

As would follow from the earlier discussion of religious intolerance, one might expect that Moral Majority supporters would be willing to use the state to curtail the free expression of diverse ideas and
the rights of minority groups. This was found to be true, but supporters were not very different from others on these matters.

What we found was that commitment to traditional moral
norms, collectively called "social traditionalism" (Himmelstein 1983),
was the strongest link among the supporters of the Moral Majority. A
high score on the social traditionalism scale meant support for traditional sex roles and school prayer, believing in the importance of hard
work, and being against abortion as well as against sex education in
the schools. Moral Majority supporters were people committed to traditional moral beliefs. In other words, among followers of the Moral
Majority, the social struggle is between those holding to social traditionalism and those defending new views on abortion, sexuality, family matters, etc.

Over the past thirty years, the nature of private life has become
an emotionally charged political topic. As discussed in the Introduc-

tion, in the nineteenth century, some religious conservatives (the pre-decessors of the fundamentalists) reacted to modernization by trying to make the home a sanctuary for saintliness. But the countercultur-ists made the nature of private life a public issue. Feminists argued that gender was political and sought legal changes that would have an impact on family life. Similarly, homosexuals fought for their civil rights, and this included gaining acceptance for homosexuality as a form of private life. Not only did the counterculture claim moral rights for the self and champion aesthetic pleasures, but libertarians sought to apply their principles to the private world. The politiciza-tion of the private realm activated numerous defensive movements on behalf of traditional private morality.

A distinctive feature of the Christian Right is its willingness to use the state to enforce traditional private morality. Unlike many other fundamentalist groups, the Moral Majority and similar Chris-tian Right organizations entered politics and fought to turn their moral code into the law of the land. During the 1980s, at least, groups such as the Moral Majority were politicking in Washington on behalf of social traditionalism (Hertzke 1988). The Moral Majority was per-ceived as the public defender of social traditionalism, and this gained popular support.[2] Such an explanation raises the question: In a mod-ern society, why is a traditional moral code significant?

The Importance of Social Traditionalism

The American public is divided on traditional morality. On the issue of abortion, for example, approximately 80 percent of Ameri-cans support legalizing abortion in cases in which the woman has been raped, but only about 40 percent would give their support if the abortion is desired because the mother believes she cannot afford to have more children (Tamney 1986b; Lewin 1989). About half of all Americans agree with the statement: "It is much better for everyone involved if the man is the achiever outside the home and the woman takes care of the home and family" (Sigelman and Presser 1988:332). However, a majority of Americans support the nontraditional practice of having sex education in schools. Overall, however, there is signifi-cant support for social traditionalism.

Why do people accept social traditionalism? The Middletown project found that not only Christian Rightists held to traditionalist morality. Older people were also more likely to be traditionalists. This makes sense in that these people were raised and educated in an envi-ronment where traditional values were less often questioned. One explanation for social traditionalism, therefore, emphasizes socialization—i.e., certain types of people are likely to have been taught as children the considerable importance of the values composing the traditionalism scale (*see also* Wood and Hughes 1984; Wald, Owen, and Hill 1989a). Consistent with the previous discussion of conservatism, political conservatism has also been found to be directly related to the traditionalism scale (*see also* Wald, Owen, and Hill 1989a). But social traditionalism is accepted by younger people, by individuals not committed to the Christian Right, and by people not politically conservative. I offer, therefore, another explanation for the appeal of social traditionalism that goes beyond the data at hand. The popularity of social traditionalism is also related to its strong legitimation.

Legitimacy

Legitimacy is a term that is much used and rarely defined. It is accepted, however, that the issue of legitimacy is a basic social problem. I believe that it has relevancy to the question of why social traditionalism has appeal, as I shall make clear. First, however, it is necessary to establish what legitimacy is and what the sources of legitimacy are.

The basic meaning of *legitimacy* is the quality of lawfulness. Not all laws, however, are considered legitimate, as is illustrated by popular opinion prior to the American, French, and Russian revolutions. Moreover, something can be legitimate that is outside the purview of the law. Thus, we may say of an argument that it is legitimate, meaning that it is logical or rational. In the not-too-distant past, people referred to the legitimate theater, thereby distinguishing Broadway plays from the likes of burlesque, and later, the movies. This usage reflects the broadest meaning of legitimacy—that something is in accordance with established rules of correctness or propriety.

The notion of legitimacy, however, implies the existence of a certain kind of standard that exists in its own right—i.e., a standard that is not mere opinion or the dictate of those holding power. The sociologist Max Weber (1966:125) recognized three types of reasons for acting: expediency, habit, and legitimacy. Unlike actions that are taken because they are useful or those performed unthinkingly, legitimate acts are performed because they are felt to be "binding."

The question, then, is: What makes us believe that a rule is binding? The most obvious answer is that a person who accepts some command to be the will of God will experience the rule as binding. The sacred transcends us and is not rooted in our will, individually or collectively. A rule which has God as its source would be considered legitimate and binding because the rule's origin would be beyond our decisions. A rule binds because we did not create it; therefore, we have no choice but to obey it. Legitimacy means a rule or belief is expressive of something that has not been humanly created.

With this definition in mind, then, let us consider the sources of legitimacy. A rule justified by a supernatural source would be legitimate. But there are other sources of legitimacy. First, nature can give legitimacy. If something is considered natural, this means that it is not human-made; natural laws will remain regardless of what humans do. The law of nature is as much a source of legitimacy as the law of God. Second, history is a source of legitimacy. As the collective memory of a people, history can be the source of a concept of an ethnic or national destiny (Gordon 1971:3). Acts can be legitimated by arguing that they are part of the inevitable development of a people. Marx's class-based history of humanity is an example of a history that has been used to legitimate behavior. Similarly, it is not uncommon in today's world to hear or read about appeals by political leaders to the historic destinies of ethnic groups and nations. History can be understood as a force acting on us and moving us toward a certain fate. At any one point in time, the history of a group is over, and in that sense history is beyond our power. Of course, the interpretations of any history will vary, and this undermines the power of history to convey legitimacy. But, history has been used, and will be used, to find direction and purpose that seems to have some meaning, that seems to bind us to something beyond ourselves.

Legitimacy, then, is the search for reality, for the fixed, the eternal. Something can be legitimated by tracing it to God's will, to nature, or to historical destiny.

Legitimacy and Social Traditionalism

It is suggested that social traditionalism retains an appeal for Americans because it is a strongly legitimated ideology. First, proponents claim that traditionalist norms are based on the Bible. This contention is disputed, but undoubtedly Christian Right leaders and others like them repeatedly stress that the traditional moral code is Bible-based. Second, on issues such as family roles and homosexuality, Christian Right leaders have asserted that liberal views are unnatural, in contrast to their own norms which supposedly reflect the natural condition such as the nature of womanhood and so-called normal sexual behavior. Third, the leaders of the Right have tried to equate the national identity and their social norms. The destiny of the United States is linked to the citizens' attitudes toward traditional norms. Falwell wrote: "For America to stay free, we must come back to the only principles that God can honor: the dignity of life, the traditional family, decency, morality, and so on" (Falwell, Dobson, and Hindson 1981:27). What makes social traditionalism a powerful ideology, then, is the fact it can be and is legitimated in multiple ways consistently and frequently.

This is not to suggest that competing ideologies are not legitimated. It is beyond the scope of this work to examine the legitimacy claims of every contemporary ideology. But I do suggest that what have been called the four modern ideational sets are less strongly legitimated in people's minds than is social traditionalism. I can illustrate this issue with a comparison of some traditionalist and libertarian ideals.

Clergy in Middletown were asked their positions on eight public issues and what their reasons were for their attitudes (Johnson and Tamney 1986). Most of the reasons given by the clergy had nothing to do directly with religion—i.e., the responses did not include any mention of God, the Bible, or Christianity. It was found that conservative clergy more often used religious justifications for their issue positions. Consistent with this finding, religious reasons were most frequently given to justify two traditional positions, support for school prayer and opposition to homosexuality. Two other questions asked about issues related to libertarianism, affirmative action and the equal rights amendment. A minority of reasons given in support of the libertarian position on these issues were religious, as were some of the reasons given for *opposing* the equal rights amendment. These results mean that both libertarianism and social traditionalism are given religious justification. But the evidence also suggests that, of these two popular ideologies, it is social traditionalism that is more strongly legitimated on religious grounds.

Consistent with these results from Middletown, a commentator has noted that, in general, political liberals have avoided using religion:

> Whereas the political right has welcomed the God-talk of its religious supporters...the political left has had a morbid fear of religion encroaching on the secular realm....The doctrine of the left is that 'religion' must not lead the public debate. Instead, it must be on call to serve only when commanded by secular leaders (Wall 1986:59).

Thus, political liberals have deprived themselves of the use of a powerful legitimating mechanism.

The support for social traditionalism, then, can be explained in terms of socialization, political conservatism, and legitimation. Indirectly, these factors help us to understand the appeal of groups such as the Moral Majority. The popularity of such organizations is rooted in allegiance to traditional values. Because social traditionalism is strongly legitimated, and because the Christian Right was portrayed as the defender of a beleaguered traditionalism, the Right could claim legitimacy. This is an important social asset.

The limited but real support for Moral Majority can now be interpreted. My concern is why the Christian Right as such appealed to modern people. Three reasons have been suggested. First, political conservatives motivated by their belief that traditional morality must be inculcated in the population to preserve capitalism and social order have supported the Christian Right. Second, there are people who, at least in a time of change, personally prefer an authoritarian religion such as Christian Rightism. Third, because the Christian Right is perceived as the public defender of social traditionalism, which has broad appeal, the Christian Right was able to gain some popular support. Given the resources available to the Right and the extent of support for social traditionalism, the question arises: Why has the Christian Right not been *more* successful?

Limits to the Popularity of the Christian Right

The Fall of the Moral Majority

In 1979, the Reverend Jerry Falwell founded Moral Majority, Incorporated. Both the individual and his organization captured a great deal of media attention. In 1986, Falwell created a new organization, Liberty Federation, and Moral Majority was made a component of the Federation. The stories surrounding this event said that the change was not a retreat, that now Falwell would be able to speak out on a broader range of issues, and that the change would allow Falwell to develop a new image. But the most telling comment came from a Falwell aide: "Moral Majority is sort of being put to sleep" (quoted in Church and State 1986b:15). In November 1987, Falwell quit as president of the Moral Majority and the Liberty Federation. Donations to Moral Majority had peaked in 1984. By 1989, the financial returns from those on the organization's mailing list were not paying the administrative costs of using the list (Niebuhr 1989). In 1989, Moral Majority ceased to exist as a formal organization.

This event cannot be explained by basic changes in Falwell's ambitions. He continues to want to control the American government. It appears, however, that he now pins more of his hope on Liberty University, which he founded in 1971. He has said of this university: "We have a dream of 50,000 students shortly after the first of the century.... One day we will be doing what Harvard has done. We'll have hundreds of our graduates running for office" (Christianity Today 1986:41).

Nor can the failure of the Moral Majority be explained by any sea-change in public opinion. At least in Middletown, public opinion about the Moral Majority changed little between 1981 and 1984. This organization did not lose support. On the other hand, it never had a large following.

What did change during the 1980s was Falwell's ability to influence the general population. In 1982, a Senate race poll was done in Falwell's home state, Virginia: "28 percent of those polled said they would be 'less likely' to vote for a candidate Mr. Falwell had endorsed" (Clendinen 1985:Y13). In 1985, a similar poll found that 51 percent of those surveyed said they were less likely to vote for a candidate that Falwell endorsed (Church and State 1986b:15). Consistent with these findings, a study of the 1984 presidential election reported that Moral Majority support seemed to have lost votes for Ronald Reagan (Johnson and Tamney 1985b). Generally, Christian Right candidates for national offices did poorly (Johnson, Tamney, and Burton 1989; 1990). The Moral Majority was put to sleep because it had lost what little political influence it had.

Although the focus is on just one religious organization, the real story is the Christian Right movement. The fading away of the Moral Majority was accompanied, if not preceded, by decline in two other Christian Right organizations that came to life during the 1980s, namely Religious Roundtable and Christian Voice (Hadden 1986:39). The fate of the Moral Majority relates to what is happening to the Christian Right generally in the United States.

I shall not dwell on the fact that enthusiastic supporters of socialist and countercultural ideas strongly oppose the Christian Right. Not only is this obvious, but this antipathy can only explain a small part of the extensive opposition to the Christian Right. It is argued that the Moral Majority failed because: (1) its strategy jeopardized church self-interest; (2) its program was too inconsistent with the libertarian ideational set; (3) leaving aside values, many believe that increased church-state entanglement is dangerous for the nation; and (4) the Moral Majority lost its legitimacy.[3]

Church Self-Interest

Many fundamentalists came to believe that political involvement of the clergy jeopardized the achievement of an essential task, evangelism. Within American fundamentalism, there has always been a tension between evangelism and sociopolitical activism (Marsden 1982). It has been feared that political division among Christians hurts evangelism. On practical grounds, therefore, many religious leaders have opposed the political involvement of the clergy (Poloma 1986:334).

The Christian Right and Intolerance

Many Americans were turned off by what they considered the unfair tactics of the Christian Right. In the 1983 Middletown study, respondents who were against the Moral Majority were asked, "Are you against the goals of the Moral Majority, the methods they use to try to attain the goals, or both the goals and methods?" The responses were (n = 148): goals – 4 percent; goals and methods – 48 percent; methods only – 47 percent; against neither – 2 percent. (In addition, 15 people were not sure what they were against.) Significantly, quite a number of people opposed only the methods of Falwell and company (*see also* Zwier 1984:189–190).

Moral Majority tactics tended to misrepresent opponents, play on emotions, and in general, lack civility. For instance, at a religious meeting in 1986:

> Falwell denounced the American Civil Liberties Union (which he called the "Anti-Christian Liberties Union"), the National Organization of Women (which he called the "National Order of Witches"), and the National Education Association. Such organizations, he said, "are going day and night to throw God out of everything America stands for" (Church and State 1986a:18).

The circumvention of rational arguments in favor of emotional appeals did not win favor even among people possibly sympathetic to some of Falwell's positions. The Moral Majority was perceived as intolerant, avoiding rational arguments, even unethical.

In 1988, a bill passed in Congress that concerned civil rights. It was meant to ensure that, when anti-discrimination laws were violated by organizations, including colleges, the resulting penalties would be applied not just to the specific programs found to be discriminatory (as the courts had interpreted a previous law), but to the whole organization. Mainline Protestant groups, as well as the American Jewish Congress and the U.S. Catholic Conference, supported the law. Falwell, on the other hand, charged that the bill "is the greatest threat to religious freedom and traditional moral values ever passed." He called the bill "the Civil Rights Sodom and Gomorrah Act," because it

supposedly would force churches to "hire a practicing active homo-
sexual drug addict with AIDS to be a teacher or youth pastor" (quoted in Andrews 1988:A3). Name-calling and emotional phrases were
tactical weapons of the Moral Majority.

The Right's intolerance would, if it gained power, be institution-
alized. In the name of family rights, the Christian Right has attacked
public education. Public school teachers tend to value letting children
explore and develop on their own. This is understood to be consistent
with the pluralist nature of American society (Park 1980). However,
what educators understand as expressions of individual and academic freedom, Christian Rightists interpret to be examples of moral rela-
tivism and attacks on traditional morality. Peshkin (1986:43, 81) dis-
covered in his case study of a Christian school that obedience rather
than knowing how to learn was the desired student attribute; appropriately, teachers in this institution were supposed to act as loving
dictators. One Christian Rightist wrote: "Why should a child be
required to *examine* or *defend* what parents have taught him? And
what justification can educators offer for attempting to *change* what a
child believes?" (Morris 1980:613). And: Aren't schools promoting the
humanist belief in 'maximum individual autonomy'?... Why is the
business of schools to wean kids from the influence of their parents
and other authority figures?" (Morris 1980:614). The Rightists do not
want the schools to embody individualism and academic freedom.
Rather, they want schools to reinforce church and home.

In 1986, Christian Rightists sought, with initial success, to ban
books from a Tennessee school district. The books included *The Diary
of Anne Frank*, *The Wizard of Oz*, and *Macbeth*. Conservative columnist
George F. Will was highly critical of the plaintiffs, writing among
other things that: "Pluralism depends on tolerance of diversity, a
value subverted by assertion of a constitutional right to retreat from
all but comforting instruction" (Will 1986:8). George Bush, then Vice-
President of the United States, criticized those Christians who were
trying to censor public school libraries. In his speech, Bush warned of
the need for tolerance and the danger of using government to impose
morality on unwilling citizens (Church and State 1987a).

Freedom for the Christian Right means primarily eliminating
state control of religion and papist churches. The narrowness of the
Christian Right's defense of liberty, it is argued, has alienated many
people, including many political conservatives. Libertarianism
embraces a tolerance of dissent and an emphasis on rational dis-
course, both of which have been lacking in the Christian Right's tactics and goals.

Opposition to Church-State Entanglement

A conservative–Christian Right argument holds that contemporary society is faced with a "new barbarism" and thus the state, in alliance with religion, must defend and promulgate an ethic of anti-selfism. To better discuss this matter, I will use the concept of 'civil religion.' There is a very basic problem faced by any secular society, as was recognized long ago by Rousseau. Rousseau realized that "there is no longer, and can no longer be, an exclusive national religion; all religions that tolerate others must be tolerated, insofar as there is nothing in their dogmas contrary to the duties of the citizen" (1974:114). In such a context, Rousseau believed, the sovereign needs to establish a civil creed which, in Rousseau's opinion, would contain some basic religious beliefs. He called this creed "civil religion."

A perceived need to institutionalize a civil religion in the United States is widespread. There is growing support for moral education in the schools, and not just from political conservatives. The California State Board of Education has called for more consideration of religion in history texts. The state superintendent of public instruction said there was no intention to advocate any one religion: "We're [going to be] teaching about religion. We're not teaching religious doctrine" (San Francisco Chronicle 1987). However, one purpose of this policy change is to give more importance to the social role of ethical values such as honesty which, the superintendent claimed, are shared by nearly all religions. In the same year, New York's Governor Cuomo, a liberal, also urged that the schools teach values such as:

> compassion, a sense of personal worth, respect for each individual's rights, awareness of the equality of all Americans, an understanding of working for a common good greater than one's personal interests, respect for the law, and a love of country (Schmalz 1987:Y20).

The governor said he was responding to the problems of drug abuse, alcoholism, teenage pregnancy, and materialism.

The obvious question that arises is: In a religiously diverse society such as the United States, how is it possible for the state to support *a* civil religion? It is argued that all 'good' people and all religions share a common morality. It can then be concluded that state support for a shared morality will not divide the nation. A rather simplified analysis of morality is assumed: (1) immorality is the result of selfishness; (2) all religions emphasize the need to subordinate self-interest to a higher good; and (3) therefore, all religions share the same basic morality.

Such an analysis, however, is too simple. Governor Cuomo spoke about how morality could be taught through the use of biographies such as those of Eleanor Roosevelt and Martin Luther King, Jr. (Schmalz 1987:Y20). Meanwhile, Christian Rightists have fought to exclude a book from the public schools because it praised Dr. King and what he struggled to achieve (New York Times 1986c:E6). Once serious moral discussion starts—over the significance of the civil rights movement, for example—the absence of moral consensus in a modern society becomes obvious.

The same Mario Cuomo opposed an amendment banning abortion because it "would divide society, undermine religious toleration, and imperil the nation's pluralistic character" (Briggs 1984:13). Given these supposed consequences, and even though he is a Catholic and against abortion, Cuomo did not believe that as a government official he should push for an anti-abortion constitutional amendment. He said: "Our public morality, thus—the moral standards we maintain for everyone, not just the ones we insist on in our private lives—depends on a consensus view of right and wrong" (Cuomo 1984:9). In the absence of consensus, Governor Cuomo did not believe that public officials are obligated to seek the legalization of their religious convictions because of the political danger of such action for the continuance of the state.

The abortion controversy is only one example of the profound moral differences among Americans. In the United States, there are at least two Christian-based contenders for the American civil religion, one supported by the Christian Right and one supported by liberal Christianity (Wuthnow 1988). But this, too, oversimplifies. An Anglican Franciscan monk wrote in reference to his church: "The days of cohesive community which would accept a single moral standard are gone" (Tastard 1984:14).

The political critique of the Christian Right, then, centers on the reality of pluralism and the absence of a moral consensus in modern society. In a modern society, religious and moral diversity make it politically dangerous for a state to become identified with a religion. In the absence of consensus, the use of the state to enforce a moral code creates social conflict and disrespect for the law (Wiseman 1986; Kennedy 1984). Accordingly, government must limit itself to legislating only in rare cases where consensus does exist, or when matters are essentially public in nature and thus require state action. Out of necessity, if not conviction, the United States works with a minimalist civil religion that embodies libertarian principles such as human rights and social tolerance. Although social traditionalism, the basis of the proposed right-wing civil religion, has the advantage of being more strongly legitimated, libertarianism has the advantage of being more practical in modern societies characterized by diversity. Thus, although Americans of various political and religious persuasions want to strengthen this or that aspect of traditional morality, many of them end up committed to a libertarian-based, minimalist civil religion as a practical necessity in a modern society. As a result, the Christian Right found itself politically out in the cold.

The Loss of Legitimacy

What makes social traditionalism a powerful ideology is the fact that it can be legitimated in multiple ways. What made the Moral Majority so appealing was its willingness to forcefully carry out the task of defending social traditionalism. Attempting to increase his influence, however, Falwell moved away from the defense of social traditionalism. When the Liberty Federation was created, one of its stated purposes was to allow Falwell to speak out on a wider range of issues, such as the 'star wars' program and support for the contras in Nicaragua (Church and State 1986b:15). In fact, Falwell had already done this. I suggest that, by addressing new political issues such as star wars, Falwell lost his legitimacy. That is to say, it is much harder to justify the star wars military program than, say, traditional sexual roles, in terms of the Bible or nature or historical destiny.

Falwell also adjusted his argumentation as a means to widening his appeal:

> On most issues, whether pornography or abortion, I try to do more than just quote the Bible. You can't win a national debate from simply a scriptural perspective. So I try to come at these things from a secular [one].... (Kalter 1985:22).

Similarly, a Washington lobbyist for the Moral Majority said:

> We are not a religious organization, and we have some non-religious people who support us because of our stand for a strong national defense. We don't try to use scripture or words of Christ to convince people. If we started to use scripture we would bleed ourselves to death. We want to influence government (Hertzke 1988:89).

The nature of Falwell's arguments shifted not only because of a tactical change, but also because he broadened his political focus. In

1985, Falwell and the Reverend Jesse Jackson were interviewed by Ted Koppel on ABC's "Nightline." The subject was apartheid. At one point in the discussion, Koppel summed up his guests' remarks as follows: "You [Jackson] see it as a moral issue; you [Falwell] see it as a geopolitical issue" (USA Today 1985:A9). Falwell had just analyzed the South African issue in terms of American national security. In 1988, after Falwell praised a radio program sponsored by the Focus on the Family organization, a spokesperson for this organization commented: "Moral Majority took stands on South Africa. Man, we don't do that! Our organization is concerned with the health of the nuclear family" (Niebuhr 1989:A5).

Falwell moved away from his strengths. He shifted to issues not easily legitimated and arguments not clearly legitimate.

Conclusion

The flowering of the counterculture was followed by renewed public visibility of fundamentalism. People wondered how such an old-fashioned religion could thrive in a modern society. However, more than liberal Christianity, fundamentalism has accommodated the alternative tradition, and fundamentalist churches seem more effective at creating community and congregational loyalty. Moreover, fundamentalism has accommodated modern ideas. Now that the issue of legitimacy and the idea of civil religion have been introduced, I can add other reasons for fundamentalism's popularity.

Social traditionalism is the moral code of fundamentalism. The that fact this code is strongly legitimated must add to the appeal of fundamentalism. Moreover, because social traditionalism is strongly legitimated, I believe that it is perceived as valuable by some in the conservative elite. Social traditionalism is an appealing basis for a civil religion. Earlier in this chapter, I discussed Jeane Kirkpatrick's fear of barbarism, which resulted from her pessimistic view of human nature. Among such people, and regardless of their personal moral beliefs, social traditionalism would be seen as a useful defense against social disorder. Thus, fundamentalism has appeal in a modern society because its moral code is strongly legitimated and because it is considered useful as a basis for a civil religion.

The real mystery for social scientists is not the appeal of fundamentalism in general but the appeal of the Christian Right, which has tried to eliminate the cultural side of modernity. I have made three relevant arguments. First, political conservatives are attracted to the Christian Right. In part, this is a political strategy to divide the working class; in part, conservatives agree with the Religious Right that the state must be used to diminish selfism. Likewise, political conservatives and the Christian Right perceive the counterculture as the harbinger of a new age of barbarism. Second, authoritarian, or authority-minded, people prefer an authoritarian form of religion such as can be found in Christian Right churches. Third, the Christian Right gained some popularity as the defender of traditionalism.

Given these sources of support, the question arises: Why is the popularity of the Christian Right so limited? In my discussion, I did not dwell on the obvious fact that enthusiastic supporters of socialist and countercultural ideas will strongly oppose the Christian Right. I have elaborated on what I believe are the more important reasons why the Christian Right has had limited appeal.

First, fundamentalist leaders came to realize that political partisanship hurts church growth. Second, the intolerance evident in the Right's tactics and plans for cultural institutions such as schools was unacceptable in a society where so many people are committed to libertarianism. Third, although there is much sympathy today for the institutionalization of a civil religion, practical political considerations favor the libertarian, minimalist civil religion over the traditionalist version. Fourth, the efforts to broaden the Right's agenda and increase its political power have resulted in weakening the association of the Christian Right and social traditionalism. As a result, the Right has become less closely identified with the defense of what legitimates many people's lives.

In the Introduction, I noted that, all else being equal, state support for religion increases religious popularity. Moreover, I suggested that the state has an impelling interest in morality and therefore in religion. I have argued, however, that once one goes beyond the verbal parading of moral clichés, one does not find enthusiastic supporters of a single moral code, but rather contending moral forces. Of course, pragmatic considerations can produce a practical agreement on the need for shared rules of behavior such as laws concerning drug usage. But such rules will be a minimalist form of civil religion, expressing more the common denominator of all religions than the moral preferences of any one of them. Moreover, such rules will reflect as well the libertarian belief that ideally moral decisions are a matter for each individual. The analysis in this chapter, then, suggests that in the future there will be no return to extensive state support for religion. Thus, one of the major historical advantages of some religions in the competition of ideologies—state support—will continue to decline.

Theoretically, the study of the Christian Right highlights the importance of civil religion and legitimacy. Modern nations search for the former and all peoples yearn for the latter. The desire to feel legitimated, in turn, favors social traditionalism. This ideational set must be added to our theoretical framework. Traditionalism as it exists in the United States (and, I believe, in the West generally) obviously clashes with the countercultural themes of self-realization and the affluence ethic, but it also conflicts with libertarian ideas (for example, in the current debate over abortion). Modern societies are culturally complex and certainly not internally consistent. There is no reason to believe that—in the near future, at least—any of the ideational sets discussed in this book will disappear.

Conclusion:
The Resilience of Christianity
in the Modern World

❖ ——————————————————————————————————————— ❖

Nothing I have written means the end of religion. The need to cope with suffering and death, the search for purpose and meaning, and our inevitably incomplete understanding of life sustain religion. There will always be mystery in the world—if nothing else, a scientifically unknowable beginning and end for the world. People will always be interested in religious matters, and it seems inevitable that at least some of these people will commit themselves to a religious group. Everything I have written is simply an attempt to explain the obvious fact that in the present world specific religions in particular places vary significantly in their popular appeal.

This conclusion will: (1) elaborate on the relevance to the fate of Christianity of the theoretical framework for religious popularity presented in the Introduction; (2) summarize how the framework needs to be changed in order to explain the appeal of fundamentalism; and (3) discuss the limitations on how far Christianity will accommodate modernization.

The Original Theoretical Framework

The four propositions stated in the Introduction related religious popularity to: (1) compatibility with the irreversible aspects of modernity; (2) breadth of needs served by the social organizational carrier of a religion; (3) being part of ethnic and national identities; and (4) support from the state.

The universal and relatively irreversible aspects of modernization are technological growth, scientific development, structural differentiation, cultural pluralism, cultural differentiation, and the four modern ideational sets—libertarian, socialist, countercultural, and feminist. In a modern society, the popularity of any religion seems limited by the irreversible aspects of modernization. Secularism, desacralization, and a restricted role for churches seem to be unavoidable features of a modern society, but religious groups may limit the other two aspects of secularization—privatization and the loss of commitment—by accommodating the irreversible aspects of modernization. It has been argued throughout this work, however, that there are factors that limit such accommodation. I will return to the issue of accommodation after discussing the theoretical framework itself.

Variety of Needs Served by Christianity

A sociologist recently commented: "Religion seems to be declining everywhere in the Western world except where it possesses or acquires other work to do beyond that of relating individuals to their god" (Wallis 1986:51). Consider Chile, for example. With Pinochet in control of the Chilean government, the Catholic church played important social roles as the defender of human rights and a source of sustenance for the poor. As democracy comes to be in Chile, all this will change: "The importance of the Church is likely to be diminished, as other actors, such as the political parties, the unions, the media, and others, become more salient" (Sigmund 1986:35). To the extent that the Catholic church succeeds in winning acceptance for its social policies, it eliminates part of its appeal. As discussed in Chapter 2, this already appears to be happening in some Latin American countries such as Brazil and Nicaragua. Church leaders would probably welcome the opportunity to be concerned only about purely spiritual matters, but such a church would be less popular. If, as now seems to be happening, the world democratizes, the popularity of Christianity will probably decline.

Christianity, Ethnicity, and Nationalism

The theory says that, other things being equal, religion is more popular when it is part of an ethnic or national identity. In part, the popularity of the Polish Catholic church is a result of the incorporation of Catholicism into the Polish ethnic identity. Likewise, the Christian Right in the United States probably gains support from those nationalists who believe that Americans are God's chosen people in the contemporary world.

There are signs, however, that this source of religious popularity is problematic for the future. As was seen in the Polish case, the fusion of religion and ethnicity can lead to chauvinism, which alienates modern people. A thread that ties together all the modern ideational sets is individualism. In a sense, libertarianism, socialism, and so on all express that the individual person is important.[1] Ethnic or national chauvinism implicitly elevates the group over the individual and so contradicts the central tendency of cultural modernization.

Moreover, religion is adjusting to the emergence of a world society. Religious leaders understand both that a religion must not be identified with any one culture and that it must reach people through local cultures. They must assert the existence of a religious essence above all cultures and the equal value of all, or almost all, cultures as vehicles for communicating the essence. Missionaries of all Christian persuasions are trying to increase their appeal by using local languages, rituals, and customs. One effect of this strategy is to deemphasize the identification of Christianity with any one ethnic or national group.

One caveat is necessary, however. Nationalism and ethnocentrism are far from being spent forces in the modern world. Some religious leaders will seek to benefit from this by linking their religions to these social forces. Within a modern population, however, I suggest that this strategy will hurt as well as help, and in the long run it will be self-defeating.

Christianity and State Support

A cooperative state is something many religious leaders seek. The benefits are obvious: priests are not murdered, religious mass media are allowed, and so on. To some extent, however, the negative consequences of state hostility are offset by gains if the regime itself is not popular. Repression by an illegitimate government may create sympathy and support for a church.

Moreover, there is a positive relationship between state authoritarianism and the variety of needs served by religious organizations. Given that, in the contemporary world, political illegitimacy accompanies state monopolization of power, it works out that illegitimately authoritarian governments unfriendly to religion often end up creating popular religious organizations.

In any modern society, however, there is tension between the government and religion because of the state interest in establishing a civil religion. The main choice seems to be between a minimalist version, shaped primarily by pragmatic considerations, and an ethical code founded in a religious tradition. Political conservatives are inclined toward the latter.

A conservative government devoted to economic prosperity is faced with several threats. First, traditional cultures embed economic considerations in larger structures of social obligations such as familial duties. Second, socialist movements place social justice ahead of pecuniary gain. And third, the counterculture defines the good life in other than economic terms. I suggest that governments may find Christiani-

ty useful in coping with traditional cultures, because there is an affinity between the moral universalism of this religion and the economic
rationalism of modern economies. However, to the extent that Christianity adjusts to socialism and the counterculture, this religion will
not be very useful to states that measure success in terms of the gross
national product. Of course, a government could favor the religious
Right, which is struggling to avoid accommodating socialism and the
counterculture. This course of action does not ensure success, however, because the majority of modern people tend not to be attracted to
the rightist variant of a religion. Thus, although it is possible that in the
early stages of modernization conservative governments might find
support of Christianity to be useful, with affluence and the accompanying secular changes and liberal religious adjustments, conservative
governments will find less reason to support this religion.

Moreover, in a modern society, practical problems follow from
identifying the state with a specific religious tradition. A government
that took this course would discover that there is no moral unity even
among members of a single religion. Thus, the government's failure
to accept cultural diversity could threaten social order. The Christian
Right "sees the state imposing a coherent ideology which it calls 'secular humanism.' This is profoundly mistaken. What is actually
imposed (and that term already suggests an inappropriately directed
and conscious cause) is not so often the alternative dogma but the
dogma of alternatives" (Bruce 1989:185). Moreover, state support for a
particular tradition will not be welcomed by all within that tradition;
some will fear government control as well as the loss of potential converts over political differences. For these reasons, it seems likely that
all governments will move toward using minimalist forms of civil
religion. Thus, I suggest that, in the long run, state support for Christianity will decline in importance.

In summary, I am suggesting that if we use the original theoretical
model, and if we accept my conclusions concerning religious ties to ethnic and national identities as well as my comments on the future of state
support, and given the uncertainty about how varied the social functions of religious groups will be in the future, then we arrive at the idea
that in the future the popularity of Christianity will be heavily dependent on whether and how this religion accommodates modernity.

The Popularity of Fundamentalism

As the American fundamentalist movement illustrates, traditionalist religion is not a unified social movement. Of course, the same is
true of liberal religion. I find these categories useful, but in fact there

exist not seperate religious types but a religious continuum. For instance, many fundamentalists have accommodated modernity to some meaningful extent. Given this change, the popularity of fundamentalism is readily understandable. However, there are reasons why fundamentalism as such is appealing. To understand this appeal, we need to consider: (1) two ideational sets other than the modern ones—namely the alternative tradition and social traditionalism; (2) the affinity between traditionalist religion and political conservatism; and (3) authoritarianism.

Modern culture has not replaced traditional culture; rather, modern ideas gain social dominance while being periodically critiqued from a traditional point-of-view. A modern society accumulates ideas. It is full of avant-garde art stores as well as museums. Ancient ideas lose their importance but not their existence. Especially in times of cultural turmoil (such as the sixties), ancient traditions resurface and attract attention. The alternative tradition represents a world view so different that it cannot be absorbed into modern culture. It remains outside established cultures.

Similarly, modernity does not mean—in the short run, at least—the abandonment of social traditionalism (i.e., whatever is considered the traditional morality in a culture). In part, this is because the socialization process, anchored in primary relationships, will continue to pass on seemingly outdated ideas. In part, because traditional ideas are generally more likely to be perceived as legitimate than modern ones, they endure long into a process of change. Traditional moral codes are more likely to be found in classical religious sources, to be consistent with people's concept of nature, and to be part of some group's vision of its historic destiny. The first point is true because it is unlikely that modern ideas will be specifically stated in any old texts, including religious ones. The second point is true because ideas about what is natural would have been shaped by old religious ideas (and vice versa). Regarding the third point, ideas of destiny are by nature rooted in the past. Thus, compared to modern moral codes, social traditionalism is more likely to be legitimated as supernaturally ordained, as based on nature, and as part of the historical identity of a people. Because legitimacy is important to people, and because traditional codes more than modern ones are likely to be perceived as legitimate, social traditionalism will persist in a modern society.

The alternative tradition and social traditionalism are quite different entities. While the former is premodern, the latter is from an earlier stage of modernization. It is more meaningful to view new moral developments as contradicting social traditionalism rather than the alternative tradition because what are perceived as traditional and new moralities express different ways of interpreting the same religious and moral heritage. Conceivably, new moral ideas will displace traditional ones yet leave alternative ways in place. In any case, the present social situation includes both the alternative tradition and social traditionalism—the former because it is a morsel contemporary culture cannot swallow, the latter because it is so strongly legitimated.

This analysis suggests that two propositions must be added to the model.

Proposition 5: A religion will be popular to the extent that it accommodates the alternative tradition and social traditionalism.

Proposition 6: The relative importance of any ideational set in affecting religious popularity depends on its degree of legitimation. Traditionalist religion does accommodate these old ideational sets more than liberal religion, which accounts in part for the continued popularity of fundamentalism.

As I alluded to earlier, there are affinities among traditionalist religion, the alternative tradition, and political conservatism. To begin with, I consider the first two, traditionalist religion and the alternative tradition. The most direct and complete responses to the alternative tradition in the United States were the Jesus movement and charismatic Christianity, responses rooted more in traditionalist than in liberal religion. I suggest this could happen because there is an underlying similarity between fundamentalism and the alternative tradition. Both deemphasize the individual self. Of course, there are also significant differences. Whereas fundamentalists will go so far as to condemn selfism, alternative people will tend to perceive the individual self as an illusion. Whereas fundamentalists may become hostile toward the Leftists, alternative people would tend to see them simply as shallow. Yet there is an affinity between fundamentalism and the alternative tradition because neither ideational set is rooted in the current phase of modernization.

Among political conservatives there is an attraction for a specifically traditionalist form of civil religion. Conservatives want to preserve the work ethic and are fearful of radical change; they refer to a new barbarism and the possibility of social chaos. Conservatives view with concern the rise of self-oriented ideologies and of social schemes for a better world. This mentality is shared with religious traditionalists.

A well-known American evangelical theologian, Carl F. H. Henry, criticized Liberation Theology as not being authentically Christian. Among his observations about this theology were the following:

Liberation theology is utopian; it promises more than it can deliver. It views human effort as able to bring about universal justice prior to the eschatological end-time. Brevard Child criticizes liberation theology's failure to acknowledge 'the basic inability of all human schemes to accomplish genuine freedom!'

Their emphasis that evil social structures account for the economic plight of the poor, alongside the virtual suppression of a doctrine of universal sinfulness, and the consequent implication of the essential goodness or historical perfectibility of all human persons, further reflects utopian optimism about social change (Henry 1986:102–103).

Another evangelical writer found our society threatened by New Age ways, "ways that glorify the self, deny the reality of human depravity, and hold out pure, contentless experience as ultimate truth and the final arbiter of meaning and value" (Burrows 1986:22). This mentality is shared by political conservatives and religious traditionalists. Both groups tend to favor social traditionalism because this moral code emphasizes self-restraint and the necessity of conformity to supposedly time-honored conventions. Thus, it is reasonable to expect political conservatives to try to strengthen traditionalist religion.

The affinity between the alternative tradition and traditionalist religion resembles the affinity between the latter and political conservatism. All of these ideational sets play down individualism. Whether it is believing that the self is really a part of a spiritual whole, or that the individual must be subordinate to a Biblical tradition or a preestablished social order, the end result is to downgrade the significance of the individual. Of course, this is not to say that these three ideational sets are all the same. In traditionalist Christianity, for example, it is believed that each individual is created in the likeness of God, which is a basis for valuing each unique person. Thus, individualism receives more support from traditionalist Christianity than from religions that express the alternative tradition. Again, political conservatism differs from the alternative tradition in its valuing of an individualistic economic system. Yet it is also true that—relative to liberal religion—the alternative tradition, political conservatism, and traditionalist religion share an anti-modern tendency.[2]

The unique appeal of fundamentalism, then, results from its affinities with the alternative tradition and political conservatism and from its identification with social traditionalism.

In the United States, the Christian Right tried to mobilize traditionalistic Americans into a powerful political force. The aforementioned factors that favor fundamentalism gave the Christian Right reason to be optimistic. Moreover, the authoritarian nature of many Christian Right churches meant that they appealed to those people in modern society who prefer anti-libertarian social groups. This movement failed for reasons discussed in the preceding chapter. Given the bases of appeal available to fundamentalism, however, a more successful religious political movement aligned with this religious form would not be a surprise occurrence.

Limitations on Liberal Accommodation

I shall concentrate on the accommodation of liberal Christianity to the libertarian, socialist, and countercultural ideational sets. As I have said, the relation between religion and feminism is also important, but is beyond my expertise, so it shall not be considered.

Limits to the Accommodation of Libertarianism

Within Christianity, it is the Catholic church that most clearly suffers problems because of a failure to accommodate libertarian values. This has already been discussed in relationship to Poland and Latin America, but the problem is worldwide. For instance, a 1987 survey of American Catholics found "a majority of American Catholics wanting more democratic decision-making at local, diocesan, and Vatican levels" (D'Antonio et al. 1989:189).

What is at issue is not only church polity. Both the Catholic church and the Christian Right are willing to use the state to enforce social traditionalism, which means passing laws controlling what is now considered private life—e.g., sexual behavior and mass media entertainment. Because libertarianism includes minimizing the role of the state, there is a general reluctance on the part of libertarians to look with favor on increasing state control over behavior that has just come to be defined as private and belonging to individuals. Thus, libertarians support the minimalist civil religion discussed in Chapter 5 and tend to oppose state control of private life.

There are limits on how much any religious group can accommodate libertarianism. In the Western tradition, what it means to be free has come to have different denotations. Freedom denotes self-sufficiency, spontaneity, and participatory democracy. No religion is likely to provide all three ways of being free. In short, the multiple meanings of freedom produce multiple forms of a religion, thereby limiting the popularity of any one religious group.

From the point of view of maximizing freedom, it would be ideal for each religious group to be democratic. However, as previously discussed, some people in a modern society (perhaps appropriately labeled in personality terms as authoritarian) prefer a nondemocratic religion. Moreover, Americans generally seem to prefer spontaneity to democracy in church. The degree to which this is true was explained as a consequence of the religious institution playing a compensatory role in modern society. That is, given the bureaucratic nature of public life, spontaneity in church services is refreshing and a welcome balance to the rest of our public existence.

Moreover, as discussed in Chapter 4, to some extent churches can get away with not being libertarian by providing community. Again, this is related to the role assigned churches in a modern society. The institutional division of labor that characterizes modern society releases churches from having to be shining examples of participatory democracy. Although I have emphasized that modernization includes the belief in the dignity of the person and the importance of individual freedom, it is also true that as people have modernized they have become nostalgic about some real or mythic time when everyone felt part of a community. The result has been a new self-consciousness about a need for community, which gets expressed in sporadic attempts to create experimental communities outside the main structures of society and efforts to use the secondary institutions such as the churches to satisfy, if only partially, the desire for communion. Modern people yearn for community, and this contributes to determining religious popularity. At the same time, when churches focus on the community issue, they may create tension within congregations because of the lack of attention to democracy.

In summary, while Catholicism and the Christian Right are suffering the most from the failure to accommodate libertarian ideas, it is probably true that no Christian church will ever fully embody libertarian values. The social cost of this may not be great, however, as long as people associate churches more with community than with freedom, and more with spontaneity than with democracy. Finally, given the multiple ways of expressing freedom, it is not likely that any one religious group will ever fully satisfy modern people's desire to be free.

Limits to the Accommodation of Socialism

During the past one hundred years, socialist movements have been a major problem for religions. Churches have responded by trying to adopt some socialist ideals and values, hoping to capture the commitment of the working class. The Catholic church illustrates that significant doctrinal changes have and are occurring within Christianity as Christian leaders increasingly perceive the world from the viewpoint of the less powerful. In his 1988 encyclical entitled "The Social Concerns of the Church," Pope John Paul II severely and equally criticized structures based on "the all-consuming desire for profit" and structures based on "the thirst for power." The encyclical is critical of both "liberal capitalism" and "Marxist collectivism" (New York Times 1988:Y4). Distancing the church equally from the two systems is new in Catholic social doctrine.

However, there are limits to the degree that Christian leaders are likely to accommodate socialist ideas. First, the accommodation of socialist movements and churches is limited by the need for both to be concerned about their own organizational interest. In his 1988 encyclical, the pope in effect said that the church will support governments that aid human development *and* ensure that the church is protected:

> For the Church does not propose economic and political systems or programs, nor does she show preference for one or the other, provided that human dignity is properly respected and promoted, and provided she herself is allowed the room she needs to exercise her ministry in the world (New York Times 1988:Y4).

In the case of the churches, this concern about the institution means a willingness at times to compromise support for change-oriented socialist movements in exchange for benefits received from the powerful—i.e., the state or the rich. The obvious fact is that, when religion sides with the poor, churches are more likely to demand of the affluent that they surrender some of their wealth. But at the present time religions offer as the only reason for the cooperation of the rich and powerful the church leaders' claim that religion requires this sacrifice. Bishop Romero's plea that everyone identify with the lower classes is an example. This is a weak argument, and counter-interpretations of religious doctrine have arisen. The basic problem is that contemporary Christianity offers the rich and powerful little this-worldly incentive for change. Thus, strong resistance to socialist-like ideas can be expected, with the result that, out of self-interest, churches will compromise on socialist issues.

The second obstacle to the accommodation of socialism and Christianity concerns conflict. To varying degrees, socialist movements accept the pragmatic need for social conflict. While Solidarity presented a pluralistic model, the Liberation Theologians were more likely to use the phrase "class conflict." In both cases, however, the leaders perceived a social world composed of diverse groups with incompatible interests. In contrast, the Catholic church sees itself (and to some extent the state as well) as a defender of the common good. I do not believe that this view is unique to Catholicism. Churches perceive themselves as peacemakers. Religious leaders tend to believe that their message, and consequently their organizations, transcend social divisions. To engage in conflict is to surrender this self-understanding.

A third obstacle to the religious accommodation of socialism is also related to the religious organization's self-perception as transcending society. Each religion believes that its message is equally valid and relevant for every person in a society. Christian leaders tend not to accept that their religious message favors any particular group such as a social class. Similarly, these leaders tend to refuse to be associated with any particular social group. Thus, it is difficult for Christianity to become the champion of any group, such as the poor.

Several times I have had to discuss the topic of community. It is an important value in the alternative tradition and finds expression in the love imagery that is such an important part of Christianity. In the aftermath of the sixties, people were less interested in finding freedom than in feeling community in their churches. It was argued that the religious institution in a modern society must compensate for the alienation experienced in other public institutions. The self-image of churches as being above society must be seen, at least in part, as in continuity with the long-standing linkage of religion and communion.

Of course, churches do not in fact remain above conflict even when that is their self-image. For example, institutional self-interest has led the Catholic church to compromise its policy on political partisanship. In May 1987, the pope implicitly supported a pastoral letter by Italian bishops that was publicly interpreted as an endorsement of the Christian Democratic Party, which has a pro-Vatican orientation (Church and State 1987b: 141). The church's current policy on political involvement of the clergy seems unrealistic, possibly hypocritical. The problem results from the church's unwillingness to publicly acknowledge that, to some extent, its actions are determined by the desire to protect church interests. As a result, the popular appeal that might be a reward for being above political dirty work is jeopardized by the church's political defense of its resources and privileges.

The accommodation of socialism and religion is not an equally significant issue in all parts of the world. This problem probably affects religious popularity most in Eastern Europe and the third world. But even within developed countries, socialist unions or political parties have some importance—except in the United States. What distinguishes the United States is how little the poor care about socialist ideas and practices. However, now that Liberation Theology is influencing both Protestant and Catholic American leaders, the churches may popularize socialist ideas among the American poor (Cox 1987:10; Berryman 1988). Thus, even in more affluent societies churches can expect pressure to accommodate socialist ideals.

In summary, the accommodation of Christianity to the socialist ideational set is limited by the need for religious leaders to promote their group's self-interest, by the avoidance of conflict models of society on the part of religious people, and by the self-perception of religious people that their religions transcend social distinctions.

Limits to the Accommodation of the Counterculture

Because religious accommodation of the alternative tradition and of libertarianism has already been discussed, this section will refer to the relatively new elements in the counterculture, the self-realization ideal and the affluence ethic. These ideas represent an affirmation of the self as well as pleasure and beauty. As such the new cultural ideas in the counterculture are an implicit challenge to any form of Christianity.

Christianity has moved to accommodate this latest ideational component of modernization, but there are limits to the extent that such accommodation can go. As already discussed, religion is associated with community in contemporary society. Thus, even within the liberal form of Christianity, although religion allows for attention to be devoted to developing the self, yet it retains the primacy of the community.

Moreover, the concept of sinful human nature limits theological enthusiasm for self-actualization as an overriding moral norm. Although not all liberal religions have the concept of sinful nature, the belief that nature must be harnessed and viewed suspiciously is widespread:

> There is no doubt that in one form or another, Socrates and Buddha, Jesus and St. Paul, Plotinus and Spinoza, taught that the good life is impossible without asceticism, that without renunciation of many of the ordinary appetites, no man can really live well (Lippmann 1929:155).

The prevalence of ascetic rules, no matter how mild, places the counterculture in conflict with many, if not all, forms of liberal religion.

The belief in an 'animal' part of human nature predisposes Christian theologians to distrust natural desires and to favor ethical codes. Even assuming a purely positive human nature, however, theologians do not believe that conflict and harm are avoidable without a shared commitment to certain ethical principles. Thus, within Christianity, the self-realization ideal is subordinated not only to the creation of community but also to the attainment of a shared commitment to an ethical code.

Another obstacle to accommodating the counterculture relates to the understandable reluctance of any religious leader to limit religious relevancy. When it promotes the significance of beauty and pleasure, the counterculture in effect widens the part of life that would be religiously neutral. Liberal Christian leaders no doubt will continue to accept the importance of these values. But this must be troublesome. During the early phase of modernization, technology and science created a religious neutral zone. Now the counterculture seeks to enlarge this zone. Even liberal Christians must worry about how far this process will go and about how big the religious neutral zone will become. Voltaire once said, "The best is the enemy of the good." The desire for the best things and the most expanding experiences can lead people to 'forget' their moral values.

In summary, accommodation of the counterculture is limited by the greater importance given community and tradition over self-realization within Christianity and by the reluctance of religious people to lose more and more turf. Accommodating the affluence ethic is especially difficult if a religion is at the same time trying to accommodate socialism. A religion simultaneously symbolized by Bishop Romero and the "Frugal Gourmet" has an identity problem.

In the long run, Christianity will have a more difficult time accommodating the counterculture or radical libertarianism than the socialist ideational set. That is to say, the critical problems for Christianity—liberal or traditionalist—lay within the upper classes of modern society. Conversely, in the long run, this religion will most easily accommodate socialist ideas. This is because both religion and socialism emphasize the common good. There is an inherent tension between religion and both libertarianism and the new elements in the counterculture because these ideational sets so strongly express individualism. In his 1987 Christmas address before 50,000 pilgrims in St. Peter's Square, Pope John Paul II gave a warning to humanity:

> Never as much as today has man been tempted to believe
> that he is self-sufficient, capable of building with his own hands

his own salvation. This is why the Church this Christmas, once
again and with more strength than ever before, lifts her voice to
proclaim the hidden mystery and to offer once more to modern
man the 'wonderful exchange' between what he is in his finite-
ness and the all of a God who has come to meet him (New York
Times 1987).

Religious leaders are more comfortable warning us than praising us.

Wilson designated the belief that humans can control their destiny as a central aspect of modernization: "We are committed to the
idea that we can make the future by conscious planned activity" (Wilson 1976:1). This way of thinking is part of modernization and conflicts
with the religious disenchantment with humanity. What might be
called the deep structure of modernity is a belief in the value of the
individual and a faith in human planning. Such an outlook lays uneasi-
ly with all forms of Christianity, and perhaps with all forms of religion.

In conclusion, then, there exist in the Western world significant
obstacles to the popularity of Christianity:

1. the relatively irreversible aspects of modernization with their secularizing consequences

2. a likely long-term decline in state support for Christianity (admittedly, with periodic lapses)

3. increasing separation of this religion from ethnic as well as
   national identities

4. the temptation to satisfy the yearning for community which, if
   done, increases popularity but simultaneously lessens the degree
   to which churches accommodate libertarian ideas, thus adversely
   affecting popularity

5. confusion about the meaning of freedom, which makes it difficult
   for any organization to satisfy everyone's desire to be free

6. the corrupting tendencies that accompany a need for religious
   leaders to protect and nurture their organizations

7. the deep-seated reluctance of clergy to accept a conflict model of
   church or society, thereby making it difficult for clergy to work
   with socialist-inspired movements

8. a theological aversion to valuing the self, beauty, and pleasure,
   which tends to repulse those influenced by the counterculture

In the contemporary world, any religion is pulled in diverse ways by the social changes and reactions to these changes that characterize our time. No one group will be able to make use of all the available sources of potential popular support. Thus, competition within religious traditions, as well as among traditions, is likely for the foreseeable future. As Berger (1979) has noted, one result of this overall situation is to increase the probability that people will have doubts about all the competitors, with the consequence of lessening the popularity of organized religion generally.

However, future societies will be religious. In this book I have presented a theoretical framework useful for understanding which forms of religion are likely to attract the members of those societies.

Notes

❖ ── ❖

Introduction

1. This section is based on O'Dea, 1966:80–86.

2. I could have referred to a theory of religious commitment. I prefer "popularity" because it seems a broader term. "Commitment" implies a seriousness not necessarily suggested by "popularity."

3. Roozen and Carroll (1979:39–40) identified four categories relevant to the question of church growth. This framework can also be used in reference to the more general topic of religious popularity. In their terms, this work focuses on "national contextual factors," or what might more appropriately be called "international and national contextual factors."

Chapter 1

1. E. Ciupak's (1984) exhaustive review of research on Polish youth documents further the occurrence of secularization. I am indebted to Anna Partin, who translated the source materials from Polish.

Chapter 3

1. The counterculture became associated with the sexual revolution. At least in part, this movement for greater sexual freedom was another illustration of the continuing unfolding of the libertarian revolution. The sexual revolution clearly preceded the counterculture; the former was obvious as early as the 1920s. A sociologist labeled sexual innovators the "civil libertarians in the area of sex" (Cuber 1972:116–117).

2. For many people, the locational symbol of the counterculture was the Haight-Ashbury district of San Francisco, and many teenagers were attracted to that district. Talcott Parsons (1964) had described the post–World War II middle-class youth culture as valuing irresponsibility, pleasure-seeking, romance, and independence of adult expectations and authority. There is an affinity between this youth culture and hippie culture. The Haight-Ashbury district was the site for the sometimes peaceful, sometimes destructive, coexistence of these two cultures.

3. Two prominent aspects of the sixties counterculture which I have not considered were the peace and ecological movements.

Chapter 4

1. I want to be clear about the nature of the relationship between the counterculture and religion. In part, one directly influences the other, as when theologians read the works of the humanist psychologists. In part, there is a convergence between the counterculture and religion because of some mutual influence. For example, both were affected by such events as urbanization and the spread of education. So people began to value self-realization long before the counterculture took shape, and Christian thinkers began to reexamine the nature of love prior to the appearance of humanistic psychology. My point is that certain ideas have developed in modern Western society which can conveniently be labeled 'counterculture,' and liberal Christianity is accommodating these ideas.

2. Taking a different approach, Dean Kelley (1979) has argued that mainline Protestant churches have declined in significance because they lack "seriousness"—i.e., mainline congregations have no collective purpose for which the members are willing to make personal sacrifices. Indeed, these churches are in the same position as the Roman Catholic church: having accepted the cause of social justice, they find it prudent to compromise their position. Such action could be interpreted as indicating a lack of seriousness. Moreover, because the liberal accommodation of the counterculture is limited, mainline clergy may appear uncertain or even lacking in conviction. Although the details of Kelley's argument differ from mine, his characterization of liberal Christianity is not inconsistent with my analysis.

Chapter 5

1. The category "evangelical Christianity" cuts across my distinction between liberal and fundamentalist branches of the Christian religion. Evangelicals may accept either liberal or fundamentalist theology. Among the fundamentalists, many of those who tend to accommodate modernity seem to prefer the label "evangelical" to that of "fundamentalist." In their perspective, the latter label refers only to Christians who stress the necessity of living radically separated from "the world" or to those who compose the Christian Right.

2. Wald, Owen, and Hill (1989a) have argued that support for the Christian Right is also the result of resentment over the social devaluation of a personally valued subculture. Their evidence was that "people who felt that society accorded too little respect to groups representing traditional

values—church-goers, ministers, people who worked hard and obeyed the law, people like themselves [it was a sample of Southern church members]—were indeed more positively disposed to support the agenda, organizations, and activities of the New Christian Right" (Wald, Owen, and Hill 1989a:12). Although the authors' finding is quite believable, it does not establish that a feeling of resentment is a direct cause of support for the Right. An alternative explanation for their finding is that commitment to social traditionalism caused both support for the Right and the belief that the aforementioned groups are undervalued. Thus, the relationship between the latter two variables would be spurious.

3. In discussing the failure of the Moral Majority, organizational problems can not be ignored. For example, the Moral Majority lived within the fundamentalist environment and could not escape the organizational hazards arising from a separatist mentality (Reichley 1985:28; Ammerman 1987:204). I do not emphasize these organizational problems because future Christian Right groups may be able to reach higher levels of organizational efficiency. In like manner, I have not considered the liberal counter-offensive against the Moral Majority, although this liberal reaction no doubt weakened the Christian Right (Bruce 1989).

Conclusion

1. The popular stereotype of socialism equates it with the dominance of the group over the individual. However, socialists claim that the social struggle to be free is a zero-sum game, and that, unless there is a political program to achieve social justice, the struggle will result in relatively few people achieving a great deal of individual freedom at the expense of the majority. Thus, socialism supposedly maximizes equality of freedom. Moreover, in Marx's terms, socialism goes beyond an interest in negative freedom (freedom from constraint) to include a commitment to positive freedom (having opportunities for self-development) (Bottomore 1964:243). The latter form of freedom became central to the counterculture.

2. Mannheim (Wolff 1971:152–174) contrasted traditionalism and conservatism. There is some resemblance between traditionalism and what is called the alternative tradition in the text. As Mannheim noted, in both traditionalism and conservatism, the individual is less important than in the progressive world view (*see especially* pp. 164–167).

References

Adriance, Madeleine. 1985. "Opting for the Poor: A Social-Historical Analysis of the Changing Brazilian Catholic Church." *Sociological Analysis* 46:131–146.

Ammerman, Nancy. 1987. *Bible Believers*. New Brunswick, NJ: Rutgers University Press.

Andrews, Robert M. 1988. "Ads to Seek Passage of Rights Bill." *Indianapolis News* (19 March):A3.

Ascherson, Neal. 1985. "A Sad Parable for Poland." *The Observer* (London, 29 December):7.

Ash, Timothy Garton. 1988. "Reform or Revolution?" *New York Review of Books* 35 (27 October):47–56.

Aylmer, G. E. 1986. "The Religion of Gerrard Winstanley." In J. F. McGregor and B. Reay, eds., Radical Religion in the English Revolution, 91–120. Oxford, England: Oxford University Press.

Banks, Robert. 1985. "The Church at Home." In Robin Keeley, ed., *Christianity in Today's World*, 118–119. Grand Rapids, MI: Wm. B. Eerdmans.

Bannon, John Francis, Robert Royal Miller, and Peter Masten Dunne. 1977. *Latin America*, 4th ed. Encino, CA: Glencoe.

Baumer, Franklin L. 1960. *Religion and the Rise of Scepticism*. New York: Harcourt, Brace, and World.

Bender, Thomas. 1978. *Community and Social Change in America*. New Brunswick, NJ: Rutgers University Press.

Berger, Peter L. 1979. *The Heretical Imperative*. Garden City, NY: Anchor Press.

Berryman, Philip. 1980. "What Happened at Puebla." In Daniel H. Levine, ed., *Churches and Politics in Latin America*, 55–86. Beverly Hills, CA: Sage Publications.

———. 1988. "Liberation Theology and the U.S. Bishops' Letters on Nuclear Weapons and on the Economy." In Richard L. Rubenstein and John K. Roth, eds., *Liberation Theology*, 225–246. Washington, DC: Washington Institute Press.

Bingen, Dieter. 1984. "The Catholic Church as a Political Actor." In Jack Bielasiak and Maurice D. Simon, eds., *Polish Politics,* 212–240. New York: Praeger Publishers.

Boff, Clodovis. 1986. "The Value of Resistance." In Leonardo Boff and Clodovis Boff, eds., *Liberation Theology,* 92–100. San Francisco: Harper & Row.

Boff, Leonardo. 1985. *Church: Charism and Power.* London: SCM Press.

———. 1986. "Summons to Rome: A Personal Testimony." In Leonardo Boff and Clodovis Boff, eds., *Liberation Theology,* 75–91. San Francisco: Harper & Row.

Bottomore, T. B. 1964. *Karl Marx: Selected Writings in Sociology and Social Philosophy.* New York: McGraw-Hill.

Briggs, Kenneth A. 1984. "Catholic Theologians Have Mixed Reactions to Cuomo's Notre Dame Talk." *New York Times* (17 September):13.

Brooke, James. 1989a. "Vatican Undercuts Leftist Theology in Brazil." *New York Times* (23 April):Y4.

———. 1989b. "Two Archbishops, Old and New, Symbolize Conflict in the Brazilian Church." *New York Times* (12 November):Y4.

Brown, Robert McAfee. 1986. "The 'Preferential Option for the Poor' and the Renewal of Faith." In William K. Tabb, ed., *Churches in Struggle,* 7–17. New York: Monthly Review Press.

Browning, Don S. 1980. *Pluralism and Personality.* Lewisburg, Pennsylvania: Bucknell University Press.

———. 1987. *Religious Thought and the Modern Psychologies.* Philadelphia: Fortress Press.

Bruce, Steve. 1989. *The Rise and Fall of the New Christian Right: Conservative Protestant Politics in America 1978–1988.* New York: Oxford University Press.

Brumberg, Abraham. 1983. *Poland: Genesis of a Revolution.* New York: Vintage.

———. 1989. "For the Poles, An Uncertain Road Awaits." *International Herald Tribune* (16 June):6.

———. 1990. "Anti-Semitism in Poland (Again)." *Tikkun* 5 (January/February):31–34, 93–94.

Bruneau, Thomas C. 1980. "Basic Christian Communities in Latin America: Their Nature and Significance (especially in Brazil)." In Daniel H. Levine, ed., *Churches and Politics in Latin America,* 225–237. Beverly Hills, CA: Sage Publications.

———. 1988. "The Role and Response of the Catholic Church in the Redemocratization of Brazil." In Anson Shupe and Jeffrey K. Hadden, eds., *The Politics of Religion and Social Change*, 87–109. New York: Paragon House Publishers.

Buie, Jim. 1985. "A Battle of Ideas." *Church and State* 38 (September):4–6.

———. 1986. "Vouchers Are a Real Swindle." *Church and State* 39 (April):4–7.

Burrows, Robert J. L. 1986. "Americans Get Religion in the New Age." *Christianity Today* (16 May):17–23.

Burton, Ronald, Stephen D. Johnson, and Joseph B. Tamney. 1989. "Education and Fundamentalism." *Review of Religious Research* 30:344–359.

Campbell, Colin. 1971. *Toward a Sociology of Irreligion*. London: Macmillan.

Chadwick, Owen. 1975. *The Secularization of the European Mind in the Nineteenth Century*. Cambridge: Cambridge University Press.

Chaves, Mark. 1989. "Secularization and Religious Revival: Evidence from U.S. Church Attendance Rates, 1972–1986." *Journal for the Scientific Study of Religion* 28:464–477.

Christianity Today. 1986. "Where Is Jerry Falwell Headed in 1986?" *Christianity Today* 30 (21 February):39–41.

———. 1981. "The Lone Ranger of Fundamentalism." *Christianity Today* 25:1095–1100.

Chrypinski, Vincent. 1975. "Polish Catholicism and Social Change." In Bohdan R. Bocuirkiw and John W. Strong, eds., *Religion and Atheism in the USSR and Eastern Europe*, 241–255. London: Macmillan.

Church and State. 1986a. "We Will Never Abandon The Struggle...." *Church and State* 39 (March):7.

———. 1986b. "Falwell Organization Changes Its Name, But Not Its Stripes." *Church and State* 39 (February):15.

———. 1987a. "Bush, SBC's Rogers Support Separation." *Church and State* 40:64.

———. 1987b. "Italian Bishops' Politicking Gets Papal Support." *Church and State* 40:141.

Ciupak, Edward. 1984. *Religiosity of Young Poles* (In Polish). Warsaw: Ksiazka i Wiedza.

Civic, Christopher. 1983. "The Church." In Abraham Brumberg, ed., *Poland*, 92–108. New York: Vintage.

Cleary, O.P., Edward L. 1985. *Crisis and Change*. Maryknoll, NY: Orbis Books.

Clendinen, Dudley. 1985. "Virginia Polls and Politicians Indicate Falwell Is Slipping in His Home State." *New York Times* (24 November):Y13.

Clines, Francis X. 1989. "Izvestia Reports Polish Political Changes in Detail." *New York Times* (7 April):Y4.

Condran, John G., and Joseph B. Tamney. 1985. "Religious 'Nones': 1957 to 1982." *Sociological Analysis* 46:415–424.

Cox, Harvey. 1969. *The Feast of Fools*. New York: Harper Colophon Books.

———. 1984. *Religion in the Secular City*. New York: Simon & Schuster.

———. 1987. "A Liberation Theology for North America." *The World* 1 (January/February):9–11.

Cuber, John. 1972. "How New Ideas about Sex are Changing Our Lives." In Joann S. DeLora and Jack R. DeLora, eds., *Intimate Life Styles: Marriage and Its Alternatives*, 112–118. Pacific Palisades, CA: Goodyear.

Cumbey, Constance. 1983. *The Hidden Dangers of the Rainbow*. Shreveport, LA: Huntington House.

Cuomo, Mario. 1984. "Of Faith and Freedom." *Church and State* 37 (November):8–11.

Curran, Charles E. 1985. *Directions in Catholic Social Ethics*. Notre Dame, IN: University of Notre Dame Press.

Curry, James A., and Richard B. Riley. 1986. "Notes on Church-State Affairs." *Journal of Church and State* 28:143–166.

D'Antonio, William, et al. 1989. *American Catholic Laity*. Kansas City, MO: Sheed and Ward.

Darczewska, Krystyna. 1983. "Some Remarks on the Model of Polish Catholicism." In Witold Zdaniewicz, ed., *Religion and Social Life*, 67–72. Poznan-Warsaw: Pallottinum.

Day, Martin S. 1984. *The Many Meanings of Myth*. Lanham, MD: University Press of America.

Diehl, Jackson. 1989. "Poland's Communists Legalize the Church." *International Herald Tribune* (18 May):1,6.

Dionne, Jr., E. J. 1984. "Peruvian Bishops Toe Wary Line at Vatican." *New York Times* (10 October):4.

———. 1986. "Nicaragua, At Vatican, Defends Bishop's Expulsion." *New York Times* (20 July):Y6.

Dodson, Michael. 1986. "Nicaragua: The Struggle for the Church." In Daniel H. Levine, ed., *Religion and Political Conflict in Latin America*, 79–105. Chapel Hill, NC: University of North Carolina Press.

Ducey, Michael H. 1977. *Sunday Morning*. New York: Free Press.

Durkheim, Emilé. No Date. *The Elementary Forms of the Religious Life*. Glencoe, IL: Free Press.

Dussel, Enrique. 1976. *History and the Theology of Liberation: A Latin American Perspective*. Maryknoll, NY: Orbis Books.

Editors. 1982. "Solidarity Strike Bulletin No. 8." In Stan Persky and Henry Flam, eds., *The Solidarity Sourcebook*, 87–90. Vancouver, BC: New Star Books.

Elgin, Duane. 1981. *Voluntary Simplicity*. New York: William Morrow.

Ellwood, Robert S. 1973. *One Way: The Jesus Movement and Its Meaning*. Englewood Cliffs, NJ: Prentice Hall.

———. 1979. *Alternative Altars*. Chicago: University of Chicago Press.

Falwell, Jerry. 1980. *Listen, America*. New York: Doubleday.

Falwell, Jerry, Ed Dobson, and Ed Hindson. 1981. *The Fundamentalist Phenomenon*. Garden City, NY: Doubleday.

Fenhagan, James C. 1977. *Mutual Ministry*. New York: Seabury.

Ferguson, Marilyn. 1980. *The Aquarian Conspiracy*. Los Angeles: J. P. Tarcher.

Flowers, Ronald B. 1984. *Religion in Strange Times: The 1960s and 1970s*. Atlanta, GA: Mercer University Press.

Fogel, D. 1985. *Revolution in Central America*. San Francisco: ISM Press.

Fowler, Robert Booth. 1985. *Religion and Politics in America*. Metuchen, NJ: Scarecrow Press.

Gallup, George H. 1972. *The Gallup Poll: Public Opinion 1935–1971*. 3 Vols. New York: Random House.

———. 1985. *Religion in America*. The Gallup Report #236.

Geertz, Clifford. 1966. "Religion as a Cultural System." In Michael Banton, ed., *Anthropological Approaches to the Study of Religion*. New York: Frederick A. Praeger Publishers.

Geremek, Bronislaus. 1982. "Interview with Bronislaw Geremek." In Stan Persky and Henry Flam, eds., *The Solidarity Sourcebook*, 226–229. Vancouver, BC: New Star Books.

Gibson, Etienne. 1955. *History of Christian Philosophy in the Middle Ages.* New York: Random House.

Gieryn, Thomas F., George M. Bevins, and Stephen C. Zehr. 1985. "Professionalization of American Scientists: Public Science in the Creation/Evolution Trials." *American Sociological Review* 50:392–408.

Gill, S. D. 1981. "Shamanism." In Keith Crim, ed., *Abingdon Dictionary of Living Religions*, 674–677. Nashville, TN: Abingdon Press.

Goodman, Walter. 1984. "Church's Activist Clerics: Rome Draws Line." *New York Times* (6 September):1, 8.

Gordon, David C. 1971. *Self-Determination and History in the Third World.* Princeton, NJ: Princeton University Press.

Goulet, Denis. 1988. "The Mexican Church: Into the Public Arena." Unpublished paper.

Gruson, Lindsey. 1989. "Opposition Calls Strike To Pressure Noriega." *International Herald Tribune* (15 May):1.

Guth, James L. 1983. "The New Christian Right." In Robert C. Liebman and Robert Wuthnow, eds., *The New Christian Right*, 31–45. New York: Aldine.

Gutierrez, Gustavo. 1973. *A Theology of Liberation.* Maryknoll, NY: Orbis Books.

Hadden, Jeffrey K. 1986. "Taking Stock of the New Christian Right." *Christianity Today* (13 June):38–39.

———. 1987. "Religious Broadcasting and the New Christian Right." *Journal for the Scientific Study of Religion* 26:1–24.

Harder, Keith. 1985. "All Things in Common." In Robin Keeley, ed., *Christianity in Today's World*, 114–122. Grand Rapids, MI: Wm. B. Eerdmans.

Hassell, Greg. 1986. "Smith Uses Food as a Celebration." *Indianapolis News* (25 October):8.

Hausknecht, Murray. 1990. "Bensonhurst and Auschwitz." *Dissent* (Winter):100–101.

Heinlein, Robert A. 1968. *Stranger in a Strange Land.* New York: Berkley Medallion Books.

Henry, Carl F. H. 1986. "An Evangelical Appraisal of Liberation Theology." *This World* 15:99–107.

Hertzke, Allen D. 1988. *Representing God in Washington.* Knoxville, TN: University of Tennessee Press.

Hewitt, W. E. 1986. "Strategies for Social Change Employed by Communidades Eclesiais de Base (CEBs) in the Archdiocese of Sao Paulo." *Journal for the Scientific Study of Religion* 25:16–30.

———. 1989. "Origins and Prospects of the Option for the Poor in Brazilian Catholicism." *Journal for the Scientific Study of Religion* 28:120–135.

Hill, Christopher. 1975. *The World Turned Upside Down*. Middlesex, England: Penguin.

———. 1986. "Irreligion in the 'Puritan' Revolution." In J. F. McGregor and B. Reay, eds., *Radical Religion in the English Revolution*, 191–211. Oxford, England: Oxford University Press.

Hill, Samuel S., and Dennis E. Owen. 1982. *The New Religious Political Right in America*. Nashville, TN: Abingdon Press.

Himmelstein, Jerome L. 1983. "The New Right." In Robert C. Liebman and Robert Wuthnow, eds., *The New Christian Right*, 13–30. New York: Aldine.

Hobsbawm, E. J. 1962. *The Age of Revolution 1789–1848*. New York: Mentor.

Hodgson, Godfrey. 1976. *America in Our Time*. New York: Vintage.

Hoge, Dean R. 1979. "National Contextual Factors Influencing Church Trends." In Dean R. Hoge and David A. Roozen, eds., *Understanding Church Growth and Decline: 1950–1978*, 94–122. New York: Pilgrim Press.

Hoge, Dean R., and David A. Roozen. 1979. "Research on Factors Influencing Church Commitment." In Dean R. Hoge and David A. Roozen, eds., *Understanding Church Growth and Decline: 1950–1978*, 42–68. New York: Pilgrim Press.

Hornsby-Smith, Michael P. 1985. "The Emergence of Basic Christian Communities in the Philippines." Paper read at the annual meeting of the Religious Research Association.

Houriet, Robert. 1972. *Getting Back Together*. New York: Avon.

Howard, John Robert. 1969. "The Flowering of the Hippie Movement." *Annals of the American Academy of Political and Social Science* 382:43–55.

Hunter, James Davison. 1987. *Evangelicalism*. Chicago: University of Chicago Press.

Indianapolis Star. 1987. "Rain-Soaked Pope Praises Local Argentine Customs." *Indianapolis Star* (10 April):9.

International Herald Tribune. 1989. "Polish Communists Face Up to Change." *International Herald Tribune* (29–30 July):1

Jeffrey, Kirk. 1972. "The Family as Utopian Retreat from the City: The Nineteenth-Century Contribution." In Sallie TeSelle, ed., *The Family, Communes, and Utopian Societies*, 21–41. New York: Harper Torchbooks.

John Paul II, Pope. 1984. "Laborem Exercens." In Michael Walsh and Brian Davies, eds., *Proclaiming Justice and Peace*, 271–311. Mystic, CT: Twenty-Third Publications.

Johnson, Stephen D., and Joseph B. Tamney. 1982. "The Christian Right and the 1980 Presidential Election." *Journal for the Scientific Study of Religion* 21:123–131.

———. 1984. "Support for the Moral Majority: A Test of a Model." *Journal for the Scientific Study of Religion* 23:183–196.

———. 1985a. "Mobilizing Support for the Moral Majority." *Psychological Reports* 56:987–994.

———. 1985b. "The Christian Right and the 1984 Presidential Election." *Review of Religious Research* 27:124–133.

———. 1986. "The Clergy and Public Issues in Middletown." In Stephen D. Johnson and Joseph B. Tamney, eds., *The Political Role of Religion in the United States*, 45–70. Boulder, CO: Westview Press.

Johnson, Stephen D., Joseph B. Tamney, and Ronald Burton . 1989. "Pat Robertson: Who Supported His Candidacy for President?" *Journal for the Scientific Study of Religion* 28:387–399.

———. 1990. "Factors Influencing Vote for a Christian Right Candidate." *Review of Religious Research* 31:291–304.

Kalter, Joanmarie. 1985. "TV News and Religion: School Prayer and TV Evangelists." *TV Guide* 33 (16 November):20–22.

Kamm, Henry. 1984. "Vatican Censures Marxist Elements in New Theology." *New York Times* (4 September):1,6.

Kaufman, Michael. 1986a. "Solidarity is Beginning to Show the Signs of Strain." *New York Times* (22 June):E2.

———. 1986b. "Prayers and Sermons Mark Solidarity Anniversary." *New York Times* (1 September):L2.

———. 1987. "Polish Church Awaits Pope, Bewildered by Its New Vigor." *New York Times* (7 June):1,8.

Kelley, Dean M. 1979. "Is Religion a Dependent Variable?" In Dean R. Hoge and David A. Roozen, eds., *Understanding Church Growth and Decline: 1950–1978*, 334–343. New York: Pilgrim Press.

Kelsey, Morton. 1972. *Encounter With God*. Minneapolis, MN: Bethany Fellowship.

Kennedy, Senator Edward M. 1984. "Excerpts From Speech By Kennedy." The New York Times (11 September):10.

Kennedy, Eugene. 1979. "Earthrise: The Dawning of a New Spiritual Awareness." *New York Times* Magazine (15 April):14.

Kennedy, Michael D. and Maurice D. Simon. 1983. "Church and Nation in Socialist Poland." In Peter H. Merkl and Ninian Smart, eds., *Religion and Politics in the Modern World*, 121–154. New York: New York University Press.

Kirkpatrick, Jeane J. 1982. *Dictatorships and Double Standards*. New York: Simon & Schuster.

Kostecki, Marian J. 1985. "Between the Gospel and Politics: Changing Relations Between the Roman Catholic Church, Party/State, and Society in Post-War Poland." Unpublished paper.

Kozkowski, Maciej. 1987. "Church-State Relations and the Role of the Press in Poland." Public Address at Indiana University.

Kubiak, Hieronim. 1972. *Religynosc A Srodowisko Spoteczne*. Wroclaw: Polska Akademia Nauk-addziat W Krakowie, Number 26.

Lane, Jr., Ralph. 1976. "Catholic Charismatic Renewal." In Charles Y. Glock and Robert Bellah, eds., *The New Religious Consciousness*, 162–179. Berkeley and Los Angeles: University of California Press.

Laslett, Barbara. 1973. "The Family as a Public and Private Institution: A Historical Perspective." *Journal of Marriage and Family* 35:480–92.

Lernoux, Penny. 1989. "The Struggle for Nicaragua's Soul." *Sojourners* 18 (May):14–23.

Levin, Kim. 1984. "New York's Tribal Revival." *Village Voice* 29 (30 October):109.

Levine, Daniel H. 1981. *Religion and Politics in Latin America*. Princeton, NJ: Princeton University Press.

————. 1986. "Conflict and Renewal." In Daniel H. Levine, ed., *Religion and Political Conflict in Latin America*, 236–256. Chapel Hill, NC: University of North Carolina Press.

Lewin, Tamar. 1989. "Views on Abortion Remain Divided." *New York Times* (22 January):Y17.

Lewis, Lionel S., and Dennis D. Brissett. 1986. "Sex as God's Work." *Society* 23:67–75.

Lippmann, Walter. 1929. *A Preface to Morals*. New York: Macmillan.

Loranc, Wladyslaw. 1986. "The Party's Tasks in the Fight Against Clericalism." Polish News Bulletin (American Embassy, Warsaw) (11 February): I–XI (Translation of an article from a Communist journal).

Luckmann, Thomas. 1967. *The Invisible Religion.* New York: Macmillan.

Lynd, Robert S., and Helen M. Lynd. 1929. *Middletown.* New York: Harcourt, Brace, and World.

———. 1937. *Middletown in Transition.* New York: Harcourt, Brace, and World.

MacIntyre, Alasdair. 1969. "Atheism and Morals." In Alasdair MacIntyre and Paul Ricoeur, eds., *The Religious Significance of Atheism,* 31–53. New York: Columbia University Press.

Maduro, Otto. 1987. "The Desacralization of Marxism Within Latin American Liberation Theology: Some Hypotheses for Research and Reflection." Unpublished Paper.

Mainwaring, Scott. 1986. *The Catholic Church and Politics in Brazil, 1916–1985.* Stanford, CA: Stanford University Press.

Manning, Brian. 1986. "The Levellers and Religion." In J. F. McGregor and B. Reay, eds., *Radical Religion in the English Revolution,* 65–90. Oxford, England: Oxford University Press.

Marsden, George M. 1982. *Fundamentalism and American Culture.* New York: Oxford University Press Paperback.

Marianski, Janusz. 1981. "Dynamics of Change in Rural Religiosity Under Industrialization." *Social Compass* 28:63–78.

Maslow, Abraham. 1968. *Toward a Psychology of Being,* 2nd ed. New York: D. Van Nostrand Insights Book.

———. 1971. *The Farther Reaches of Human Nature.* New York: Viking Compass.

Mason, David S. 1984. "Solidarity and Socialism." In Jack Bielasiak and Maurice D. Simon, eds., *Polish Politics,* 118–137 New York: Praeger Publishers.

———. 1989. "Solidarity as a New Social Movement." *Political Science Quarterly* 104:41–58.

McCarthy, John D., and Mayer N. Zald. 1977. "Resource Mobilization and Social Movements: A Partial Theory." *American Journal of Sociology* 82:1212–1241.

McGregor, J. F. 1986. "The Baptists: Fount of All Heresy." In J. F. McGregor and B. Reay, eds., *Radical Religion in the English Revolution,* 23–64. Oxford, England: Oxford University Press.

McLeod, Hugh. 1981. *Religion and the People of Western Europe 1789–1970.* Oxford, England: Oxford University Press.

Miller, James. 1987. *Democracy Is In the Streets*. New York: Simon & Schuster.

Monticone, Ronald C. 1986. *The Catholic Church in Communist Poland 1945–1985*. New York: Columbia University Press.

Morawska, Eva. 1984. "Civil Religion vs. State Power in Poland." *Society* 21 (May/June):29–34.

Morris, Barbara M. 1980. "The Real Issue in Education as Seen by a Journalist on the Far Right." *Phi Delta Kappan* (May): 613–615.

Moustakis, Clark E. 1956. "Preface." In Clark E. Moustakis, ed., *The Self*. New York: Harper & Row.

Muncie Star. 1976. "Rightists Launch Plan to Save America." *Muncie Star* (26 April):7.

Munoz, Ronaldo. 1981. "Ecclesiology in Latin America." In Sergio Torres and John Eagleson, eds., *The Challenge of Basic Christian Communities*, 150–160. Maryknoll, NY: Orbis Books.

Navarro, Orlando. 1984. "Basic Christian Communities in San Gabriel de Aserri: 1979–1984." Masters Thesis, Ball State University.

New Statesman. 1984. "Church Gaining the Initiative." *New Statesman* 108 (9 November):23–24.

New York Times. 1984a. "Excerpts From 'Liberation Theology' Statement." *New York Times* (4 September):6.

———. 1984b. "Voters Found Uneasy Over Religion as Issue." *New York Times* (19 September):Y13.

———. 1986a. "New Vatican Document Endorses Struggle by Poor Against Injustice." *New York Times* (6 April):1,Y11.

———. 1986b. "Key Sections From Vatican Document on Liberation Theology." *New York Times* (6 April):Y10.

———. 1986c. "Do Textbooks Foster 'Secular Humanism'?" *New York Times* (19 October):E6.

———. 1986d. "Panel With Non-Communists To Advise Polish Government." *New York Times* (7 December):Y9.

———. 1987. "Pope Issues Warning on Seeking Human Salvation in Technology." *New York Times* (26 December):L3.

———. 1988. "Excerpts From Papal Encyclical on Social Concerns of Church." *New York Times* (20 February):Y4.

Newman, Barry. 1988. "Polish Church, Communist Party Search For a Workable Power-Sharing Formula." *Wall Street Journal* (12 May):18.

Niebuhr, R. Gustave. 1989. "Spent Crusade: Why 'Moral Majority,' A Force for a Decade, Ran Out of Steam." *Wall Street Journal* (25 September):A1.

O'Brien, Conor Cruise. 1986. "God and Man in Nicaragua." *Atlantic* 258 (August):50–72.

O'Dea, Thomas F. 1966. *The Sociology of Religion.* Englewood Cliffs, NJ: Prentice Hall.

Obando y Bravo, Miguel. 1986. "Nicaragua: The Sandinistas Have 'Gagged and Bound' Us." *Washington Post* (12 May):A15.

Ostrowski, Wojciech, and Jan Tomasz Lipski. 1983. "A Reply to Father Sroka." In Abraham Brumberg, ed., *Poland*, 222–225. New York: Vintage.

Palmer, Bruce. 1980. *"Man Over Money": The Southern Populist Critique of American Capitalism.* Chapel Hill, NC: University of North Carolina Press.

Park, J. Charles. 1980. "Preachers, Politics, and Public Education: A Review of Right-Wing Pressures Against Public Schooling in America." *Phi Delta Kappan* (May): 608–612.

Parsons, Talcott. 1964. *Essays in Sociological Theory,* New York: Free Press.

Pasca, T. M. 1986. "John Paul II Reads the Riot Act." *New Statesmen* 111 (3 January):16–17.

Pawlak, Antoni. 1990. "Censorship and the Church." Uncensored Poland News Bulletin (16 February):17–18.

Pawlikowski, O.S.M., John T. 1986. "The Renewed Catholic Debate on Church and State." *The Christian Century* 103:707–710.

Perrin, Robin D. 1989. "American Religion in the Post–Aquarian Age: Values and Demographic Factors in Church Growth and Decline." *Journal for the Scientific Study of Religion* 28:75–89.

Perry, Charles. 1985. *The Haight-Ashbury.* New York: Vintage.

Perry, H. Francis. 1899. "The Workingman's Alienation from the Church." *American Journal of Sociology* 4:621–29.

Peshkin, Alan. 1986. *God's Choice.* Chicago: University of Chicago Press.

Pierard, Richard V. 1985. "Religion and the 1984 Election Campaign." *Review of Religious Research* 27:98–114.

Piwowarski, Wladyslaw. 1976. "Industrialization and Popular Religiosity in Poland." *Sociological Analysis* 37:315–320.

———. 1984. "Bright Spots and Shadows of Polish Religiosity." In Josef Wolkowski, ed., *Faces of Catholicism in Poland* (In Polish). Warsaw: Biblioteka Augustinum.

Poblete, S.J., Renato. 1980. "From Medellin to Puebla: Notes for Reflection." In Daniel H. Levine, ed., *Churches and Politics in Latin America*, 41–54. Beverly Hills, CA: Sage Publications.

Poloma, Margaret M. 1982. *The Charismatic Movement: Is There a New Pentecost?* Boston: Twayne.

———. 1986. "Pentecostals and Politics in North and Central America." In Jeffrey K. Hadden and Anson Shupe, eds., *Prophetic Religions and Politics*, 329–352. New York: Paragon House Publishers.

Pomian-Srzednicki, Maciej. 1982. *Religious Change in Contemporary Poland*. London: Routledge and Kegan Paul.

Popieluszko, Father Jerzy. 1985. *The Price of Love*. London: Incorporated Catholic Truth Society.

Pravda, Alex. 1983. "The Workers." In Abraham Brumberg, ed., *Poland*, 68–91. New York: Vintage.

Quebedeaux, Richard. 1983. *The New Charismatics II*. San Francisco: Harper & Row.

Reay, B. 1986. "Quakerism and Society." In J. F. McGregor and B. Reay, eds., *Radical Religion in the English Revolution*, 141–164. Oxford, England: Oxford University Press.

Reding, Andreio. 1987. "Seed of a New and Renewed Church: The 'Ecclesiastical Insurrection.'" *Monthly Review* 39:24–55.

Reed, Irving B., Jaime Suchlicki, and Dodd L. Harvey. 1972. *The Latin American Scene of the Seventies: A Basic Fact Book*. Miami: University of Miami Press.

Rehnquist, Justice. 1985. "Excerpts From Opinions and Dissents in School Prayer Case." *New York Times* (5 June):13.

Reichley, A. James. 1986. "Religion and the Future of American Politics." *Political Science Quarterly* 101:23–47.

Reisman, David. 1961. *The Lonely Crowd*. New Haven: Yale University Press.

Richardson, Allan, and John Bowden (eds.). 1983. *The Westminster Dictionary of Christian Theology*. Philadelphia: Westminster Press.

Riding, Alan. 1987. "No Letup in Paraguay Battle for Souls." *New York Times* (1 April):Y4.

Romero, Archbishop Oscar. 1985. *Voice of the Voiceless*. Maryknoll, NY: Orbis Books.

Roof, Wade Clark, and Christopher Kirk Hadaway. 1979. "Denominational Switching in the Seventies: Going Beyond Stark and Glock." *Journal for the Scientific Study of Religion* 18:363–378.

Roof, Wade Clark, and William McKinney. 1987. *American Mainline Religion.* New Brunswick, NJ: Rutgers University Press.

Roozen, David A. 1980. "Church Dropouts: Changing Patterns of Disengagement and Re-Entry." *Review of Religious Research* 21:427–450.

Roozen, David A., and Jackson W. Carroll. 1979. "Recent Trends in Church Membership and Participation: An Introduction." In Dean R. Hoge and David A. Roozen, eds., *Understanding Church Growth and Decline: 1950–1978*, 21–41. New York: The Pilgrim Press.

Rossano, Pietro. 1981. "Christ's Lordship and Religious Pluralism in Roman Catholic Perspective." In Gerald H. Anderson and Thomas F. Stransky, C.S.P., eds., *Christ's Lordship and Religious Pluralism*, 96–109. Maryknoll, NY: Orbis Books.

Rousseau, Jean-Jacques. 1974. *The Essential Rousseau.* New York: New American Library.

Ruether, Rosemary. 1986. "The Conflict of Political Theologies in the Churches: Does God Take Sides in Class Struggle." In William K. Tabb, ed., *Churches in Struggle*, 18–31. New York: Monthly Review Press.

Ryan, Thomas. 1981. *Fasting Rediscovered.* New York: Paulist.

San Francisco Chronicle. 1987. "More Religion Ordered For State History Texts." *San Francisco Chronicle* (11 July):3.

Schmalz, Jeffrey. 1987. "Cuomo Intensifies Call for Schools to Teach Values." *New York Times* (8 March):Y20.

Schmemann, Serge. 1989. "Polish Agreement Is Seen as Putting the Economic Ball in the West's Court." *New York Times* (9 April):Y3.

Sheehan, Thomas. 1984. "The Vatican Errs on Liberation Theology." *New York Times* (16 September):E23.

Sigelman, Lee, and Stanley Presser. 1988. "Measuring Public Support For the New Christian Right." *Public Opinion Quarterly* 52:325–337.

Sigmund, Paul E. 1986. "Revolution, Counterrevolution, and the Catholic Church in Chile." *The Annals of The American Academy of Political and Social Sciences* 483:25–35.

Simons, Marlise. 1984. "Caution is Urged by Brazil Bishops." *New York Times* (4 September):6.

Smith, Brian H. 1980. "Churches and Human Rights in Latin America: Recent Trends on the Subcontinent." In Daniel H. Levine, ed., *Churches and Politics in Latin America*, 155–193. Beverly Hills, CA: Sage Publications.

Smith, Gary Scott. 1985. *The Seeds of Secularization*. Grand Rapids, MI: Christian University Press.

Sobran, Joseph. 1986. "Of God, Pluralism and Religious Traditions." *Indianapolis Star* (21 May):14.

Solidarity. 1982a. "The Movement for Self-Management." In Stan Persky and Henry Flam, eds., *The Solidarity Sourcebook*, 177–179. Vancouver, BC: New Star Books.

———. 1982b. "The Solidarity Program." In Stan Persky and Henry Flam, eds., *The Solidarity Sourcebook*, 205–225. Vancouver, BC: New Star Books.

———. 1984. *The Church in Poland Under Martial Law*. London: NSZZ "Solidarnosc" Information Office.

Sroka, S. J., Fr. Bronilaw. 1983. "The Spirit That Revives." In Abraham Brumberg, ed., *Poland*, 219–221. New York: Vintage.

Staniszkis, Jadwiga. 1989. "The Obsolescence of Solidarity." *Telos* 80:37–50.

Steinfels, Peter. 1988. "New Liberation Faith: Social Conflict is Muted." *New York Times* (27 July):Y4.

St. John-Stevas, N. 1984. "Tory Philosophy—A Personal View." In Eric Butterworth and David Weir, eds., *The New Sociology of Great Britain* 478–488. London: Fontana.

Suro, Roberto. 1987a. "Pope, on Latin Trip, Attacks Pinochet Regime." *New York Times* (1 April):1, 7.

———. 1987b. "Pope, Visiting Polish Factory, Proclaims Conditions Unsafe." *New York Times* (14 June):Y8.

———. 1988. "Pope, in Uruguay, Gives His Blessing to Polish Strikes." *New York Times* (8 May):Y1, Y8.

Syski, Jacek. 1990. "Polish Realities and Myths." Uncensored Poland News Bulletin (31 January):14–18.

Szajkowski, Bogdan. 1983. *Next to God...Poland*. London: Frances Pinter.

Szymanski, Albert. 1984. *Class Struggle in Socialist Poland*. New York: Praeger Publishers.

Tagliabue, John. 1988a. "Lech! Lech! Lech!" *New York Times Magazine* (23 October):36–46.

———. 1989a. "Poland Can Exercise Political Will, But There's No Way Out of Austerity." *New York Times* (23 April): E2.

———. 1989b. "Abortion Becomes Issue in Politics." *International Herald Tribune* (30 May):6.

————. 1989c. "Solidarity Adopts Cooperative Stance." *International Herald Tribune* (7 June):1–2.

————. 1989d. "Solidarity Leader Takes the Reins of Power, In Spirit If Not In Name." *Singapore Straits Times* (24 August):24.

Tamney, Joseph B. 1980. "Modernization and Religious Purification." *Review of Religious Research* 22:207–218.

————. 1984. "A Qualitative Analysis of Religious Ritual in Middletown: A Research Note." *Sociological Analysis* 45:57–64.

————. 1986a. "Fasting and Dieting: A Research Note." *Review of Religious Research* 27:255–262.

————. 1986b. "Religion and the Abortion Issue." In Stephen D. Johnson and Joseph B. Tamney, eds., *The Political Role of Religion in the United States*, 159–180. Boulder, CO: Westview Press.

Tamney, Joseph B., and Stephen D. Johnson. 1985. "Consequential Religiosity in Modern Society." *Review of Religious Research* 26:360–378.

————. 1987. "Church-State Relations in the Eighties: Public Opinion in Middletown." *Sociological Analysis* 48:1–16.

————. 1988. "Explaining Moral Majority Support." *Sociological Forum* 3:234–255.

————. 1989. "Fundamentalism and Self-Actualization." *Review of Religious Research* 30:276–286.

Tamney, Joseph B., Ronald Burton, and Stephen D. Johnson. 1989. "Fundamentalism and Economic Restructuring." In Ted Jelen, ed., *Religion and Political Behavior in the United States*, 67–82. New York: Praeger Publishers.

Tamney, Joseph B., Shawn Powell, and Stephen D. Johnson. 1989. "Innovation Theory and Religious Nones." *Journal for the Scientific Study of Religion* 28:216–229.

Tastard, Terry. 1984. "Cleft in Rock of Ages." *New Statesman* 108 (9 November):14.

Tawney, R. H. 1947. *Religion and the Rise of Capitalism.* New York: Mentor.

Teilhard de Chardin, Pierre. 1961. *The Phenomenon of Man.* New York: Harper Torchbook.

Thrower, James. 1971. *A Short History of Western Atheism.* London: Pemberton.

Tipton, Steven M. 1982. *Getting Saved From the Sixties.* Berkeley and Los Angeles: University of California Press.

Tischner, Jozef. 1984. *The Spirit of Solidarity*. New York: Harper & Row.

Touraine, Alain, et al. 1983. *Solidarity*. Cambridge: Cambridge University Press.

Troeltsch, Ernst. 1931. *The Social Teachings of the Christian Churches*, 2 vols. New York: Macmillan.

Uncensored Poland. 1985a. "The Primate and Father Malkowski." Uncensored Poland News Bulletin (8 May):18–23.

———. 1985b. "What Worries the Culture Minister Concerning Cultural Activities of the Church." Uncensored Poland News Bulletin (19 December):34–38.

———. 1985c. "Solidarity Report: Poland Five Years After August: Description. Lech Walesa's Foreword and Table of Contents August 1985." Uncensored Poland News Bulletin (9 October):8–13.

———. 1985d. "More on Solidarity Report: Summary of Conclusions." Uncensored Poland News Bulletin (24 October):14–18.

———. 1990. "Excerpts From Prime Minister Mazowiecki's 'State of the Nation' Speech to the Sejm, 18 January 1990." Uncensored Poland News Bulletin (16 February):9–12.

USA Today. 1985. "Topic: South Africa." *USA Today* (5 September):A9.

Vidler, Alec R. 1961. *The Church in an Age of Revolution*. Middlesex, England: Penguin.

Vitz, Paul C. 1977. *Psychology as Religion*. Grand Rapids, MI: William B. Eerdmans.

Wald, Kenneth D., Dennis E. Owen, and Samuel S. Hill. 1989a. "Evangelical Politics and Status Issues." *Journal for the Scientific Study of Religion* 28:1–16.

———. 1989b. "Habits of the Mind? The Problem of Authority in the New Christian Right." In Ted Jelen, ed., *Religion and Political Behavior in the United States*, 93–108. New York: Praeger Publishers.

Wall, James M. 1986. "A Vision of the Future, Not a Tired Agenda." *The Christian Century* 103 (22 January):59–60.

Wallis, Roy. 1986. "The Caplow-de Tocqueville Account of Contrasts in European and American Religion: Confounding Considerations." *Sociological Analysis* 47:50–52.

Ward, Tom. 1985. "Sex and Drugs and Ronald Reagan." *Village Voice* (29 January):14–16, 48.

Warszawski, Dawid. 1989. "The Convent and Solidarity." *Tikkun* 4 (November/December):29–31.

Weber, Max. 1966. *The Theory of Social and Economic Organization*. New York: The Free Press.

———. 1968. *On Charisma and Institution Building*. Chicago: University of Chicago Press.

Weintraub, Karl Joachim. 1978. *The Value of the Individual*. Chicago: University of Chicago Press.

Will, George. 1986. "Education Tailored to Parental Tastes." *Indianapolis Star* (10 November):8.

Willems, Emilio. 1975. *Latin American Culture*. New York: Harper & Row.

Wilson, Bryan. 1976. *Contemporary Transformation of Religion*. London: Oxford.

Wiseman, Jr., Thomas A. 1986. "Church-State Confusion: A Judicious Warning." *Church and State* 39 (February):18–21.

Wolfe, James. 1976. "Three Congregations." In Charles Y. Glock and Robert N. Bellah, eds., *The New Religious Consciousness*, 227–244. Berkeley and Los Angeles: University of California Press.

Wolff, Kurt H., ed. 1971. *Fromm Karl Mannheim*. New York: Oxford University Press.

Wolfe, Tom. 1968. *The Electric Kool-Aid Acid Test*. New York: Farrar, Strauss, & Giroux.

Wolnicki, Miron. 1989. "Self-Government and Ownership in Poland." *Telos* 80:63–78.

Wood, Michael, and Michael Hughes. 1984. "The Moral Basis of Moral Reform: Status Discontent vs. Culture and Socialization as Explanations of Anti-Pornography Social Movement Adherence." *American Sociological Review* 49:86–99.

Woodward, Kenneth L. 1986. "The Protestant Push." *Newsweek* (1 September):63–64.

Wuthnow, Robert. 1986. "Religious Movements and Counter-Movements in North America." In James A. Beckford, ed., *New Religious Movements and Rapid Social Change*, 1–28. Paris: Sage/UNESCO.

———. 1988. "Divided We Fall: America's Two Civil Religions." *The Christian Century* (20 April):395–399.

Yoder, Edwin. 1985. "Mr. Bennett: Provocative, But Not Persuasive." *Church and State* 38 (September):7.

Zborski, Bartlomiej. 1990. "Church and Censorship." Uncensored Poland News Bulletin (17 January):10–11.

Zdaniewicz, Witold. 1983. "The Catholic Church in Poland as the Social Fact 1982." In Witold Zdaniewicz, ed., *Religion and Social Life*, 7–60. Poznan-Warsaw: Pallottinum.

Zwier, Robert. 1984. "The New Christian Right and the 1980 Election." In David G. Bromley and Anson Shupe, eds., *New Christian Politics*, 174–194. Macon, Georgia: Mercer.

Index

DATE DUE

HIGHSMITH 45-220